HBJ BOOKMARK READING PROGRAM, EAGLE EDITION

Margaret Early

Elizabeth K. Cooper

Nancy Santeusanio

Level 8

Widening Circles

- WIDENING CIRCLES
  RING AROUND THE WORLD

Harcourt Brace Jovanovich, Publishers

Orlando   New York   Chicago   San Diego   Atlanta   Dallas

Cover: Russell Kelly/Focus on Sports

Printed in the United States of America   ISBN 0-15-331258-0

ACKNOWLEDGMENTS: For permission to reprint copyrighted material, grateful acknowledgment is made to the following sources:

Addison-Wesley Publishing Company, Inc.: "The Secret Song" from *Nibble, Nibble* by Margaret Wise Brown, A Young Scott Book. © 1959 by Margaret Wise Brown. Adapted from *A Time for Sleep: How the Animals Rest* by Millicent Selsam (retitled: "How Animals Rest"), A Young Scott Book. © 1953 by Millicent Selsam.

William Rossa Cole, and Sheldon Vidibor, Inc.: "The Lazy People" by Shel Silverstein from *Oh, How Silly!* edited by William Cole. Copyright © 1970 by Shel Silverstein.

Coward, McCann & Geoghegan, Inc.: Adaptation loosely based on "The People Downstairs" from *The People Downstairs and Other City Stories* by Rhoda W. Bacmeister (retitled: "The Person Downstairs").

Thomas Y. Crowell Publishers: "Way down South . . .," text only, from *Rainbow in the Morning* by Carl Withers and Alta Jablow. Copyright © 1956 by Carl Withers and Alta Jablow. An Abelard-Schuman Book.

Curtis Publishing Company: "A Letter in a Bottle," an adaptation of "A Letter by Bottle Post" by Emily Rhoads Johnson from *Jack and Jill* Magazine. Copyright © 1968 by The Curtis Publishing Company.

Doubleday & Company, Inc.: Adaptation of *The Man Who Didn't Wash His Dishes* by Phyllis Krasilovsky. Copyright 1950 by Phyllis Krasilovsky.

Benjamin Franklin Literary & Medical Society: "The Elephant's Nose" by Laura Arlon from *Humpty Dumpty's Magazine for Little Children.* Copyright 1968 by The Better Reading Foundation, Inc.

Harcourt Brace Jovanovich, Inc.: Adapted from "Little Hatchy Hen" in *Grandpa's Farm* by James Flora. © 1965 by James Flora. "Primer Lesson" from *Slabs of the Sunburnt West* by Carl Sandburg. Copyright 1922 by Harcourt Brace Jovanovich, Inc.; copyright 1950 by Carl Sandburg.

Harper & Row, Publishers, Inc.: Adapted from *The Secret Three* by Mildred Myrick. Text © 1963 by Mildred Myrick. Adapted text of *Hill of Fire* by Thomas P. Lewis. Text copyright © 1971 by Thomas P. Lewis.

Houghton Mifflin Company: Salt Boy by Mary Perrine, illustrated by Leonard Weisgard. Copyright © 1968 by Mary Perrine. Copyright © 1968 by Leonard Weisgard.

Little, Brown and Company: "The Panther" from *Verses From 1929 On* by Ogden Nash. Copyright 1940 by The Curtis Publishing Company. First appeared in the Saturday Evening Post, 1940.

Macmillan Publishing Co., Inc.: "Swift things are beautiful" from *Away Goes Sally* by Elizabeth Coatsworth. Copyright 1934 by Macmillan Publishing Co., Inc.; renewed 1962 by Elizabeth Coatsworth Beston. "Night" from *Collected Poems* by Sara Teasdale. Copyright 1930 by Sara Teasdale Filsinger; renewed 1958 by Guaranty Trust Co. of New York, Executor.

McGraw-Hill Book Company: From *Discovering Dinosaurs* by Glenn O. Blough. Copyright © 1960 by Glenn O. Blough.

William Morrow & Company, Inc.: Adaptation of pages 18–35 (text only) in *Ookie, The Walrus Who Likes People* by William Bridges. Copyright © 1962 by William Bridges.

Parents' Magazine Enterprises, Inc.: "City Street" by Vivian Gouled from *Humpty Dumpty's* Magazine. Copyright © 1971 Parents' Magazine Enterprises, a division of Gruner + Jahr, U.S.A., Inc.

Simon & Schuster, a division of Gulf & Western Corporation: Adaptation of "Dulary" from *Inside the Zoo* by Morris Weeks, Jr. Copyright © 1970 by Morris Weeks, Jr.

William Jay Smith: "There was a Young Man on a plain" from *Mr. Smith and Other Nonsense* by William Jay Smith, published by Delacorte Press, 1968. Copyright © 1968 by William Jay Smith.

Western Publishing Company, Inc.: "Comets" adapted from *Astronomy: Our Sun and Its Neighbors* by Jene Lyon. © 1974, 1966, 1957 by Western Publishing Company, Inc.

Karen Ackoff: 9–16; Richard Brown: 107; Clark Carroll: 222–223, 227; Victoria Chess: 249–250; Gil Cohen: 119–128, 131; Daily: 8, 109–118; Len Ebert: 205–210; Frank Fretz: 150–156; Michael Garland: 193; Joan Goodman: 180–189; John Hamberger: 133–139, 243–248; Blake Hampton: 168–174; Meryl Henderson: 75, 77–79, 82; John Killgrew: 108, 161, 175, 178; Jared Lee: 40–42, 55–71, 76, 103–106, 177, 179, 190–192, 251–256; Ken Longtemps: 17–20; Jon McIntosh: 176; Beth McNally: 81; Mike McNelly: 132; Sal Murdocca: 21–29; John Murphy: 199, 202; Wally Neibart: 162–167; Michael O'Reilly: 7; Irene Roman: 194–195, 229; Robert Shore: 234–242; Michael Sullivan: 228, 231; Kyuzo Tsugami: 43; James Watling: 83–94, 211–220; Jenny Williams: 45–54.

Pages 30–34, Leonard Kamsler, Ringling Bros. and Barnum & Bailey Circus; 35, The New York Times; 36–39, Leonard Kamsler, Ringling Bros. and Barnum & Bailey Circus; 44, Grant Heilman; 95, Hans Namuth; 96, Copyright © 1971, by Andrew Wyeth, Private Collection; 97, Grandma Moses: *The Old Oaken Bucket.* Copyright © 1946, renewed 1974. Grandma Moses Properties Co., New York; 98, The Metropolitan Museum of Art, Samuel D. Lee Fund, 1939; 99, Collection, The Museum of Modern Art, New York. Mrs. Simon Guggenheim Fund. Photograph by Geoffery Clements, NYC; 100, The Metropolitan Museum of Art, Gift of Edgar Williams and Bernice Chrysler Garbisch, 1962; 101, The Roland P. Murdock Collection: Courtesy, Wichita Art Museum, Wichita, Kansas; 102, Editorial Photocolor Archives; 129, Franklin Williamson/Philadelphia Zoological Garden; 140–149, Rod Brindamor, Copyright ©, National Geographic Society; 196, Ray Manley/Shostal; 197 (top), E. Cooper/Shostal; 197 (bottom), R. Ruhoff/Shostal; 198, D. Dietrich/Shostal; 200, Natalia Zunino; 201, G. Ahrens/Shostal; 203 (top right), Dr. Julius Weber; 203 (bottom left), Roger Appelton/Photo Researchers; 203 (bottom right), Shostal; 204, Ray Manley/Shostal; 221, Tim Kilby/DPI; 222, Courtesy, The American Museum of Natural History: Hayden Planetarium; 223, Grant Heilman; 224, Courtesy, The American Museum of Natural History: Hayden Planetarium; 225 (top), Runk Schoenberger/Grant Heilman; 225 (bottom), NASA; 226, NASA; 227, Wide World; 230, Dr. Leo Connolly; 232 (all 3), Mount Wilson and Las Campanas Observatories (Mount Wilson Observatory photograph); 233 (top), Mount Wilson and Las Campanas Observatories (Mount Wilson Observatory photograph); 233 (bottom left), The Granger Collection; 233 (bottom right), Courtesy, The American Museum of Natural History: Hayden Planetarium.

Contents

Try, and Try Again

Oh, For a Book

Oh, for a book and a shady nook,
    either indoors or out;
With green leaves whispering overhead
    or the street cries all about.
Where I may read all at my ease
    both of the new and old,
For a jolly good book whereon to look
    is better to me than gold.

ANONYMOUS

8

ALL STORIES ARE ANANSI'S

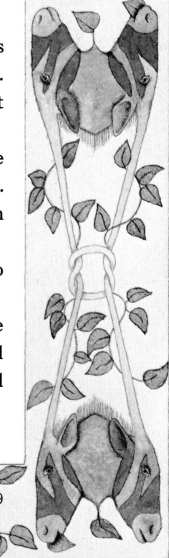

When it is story-telling time in the lands of Africa, shouts go up from the children. "Anansi, Anansi, the spider; tell about Anansi!"

When it is storytime in other parts of the world, shouts go up from the children. "Anansi, Anansi, the spider; tell us an Anansi story!"

Yes, children all over the world want to hear stories about Anansi the spider.

There are many stories about Anansi the spider. There is even a saying in Africa: "All stories are Anansi's." But long ago that had not been so.

Listen!

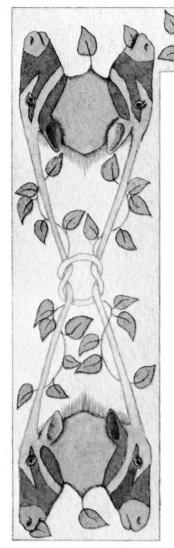

Long ago the chief god owned all the stories. Anansi had no stories at all. He wanted them, though. Oh, yes, Anansi the spider wanted all the stories to be about Anansi the Spider.

So he went to see the chief god of his people because the gods did magic. They could make anything happen. They could even grant a wish like Anansi's — that's what the stories say.

Anansi didn't go walking softly and slowly up to the chief god. Not he! He marched up to the god's house as if the place were his own.

"I want to own the stories people tell," Anansi said. "All the stories should be called Anansi the Spider stories from now on."

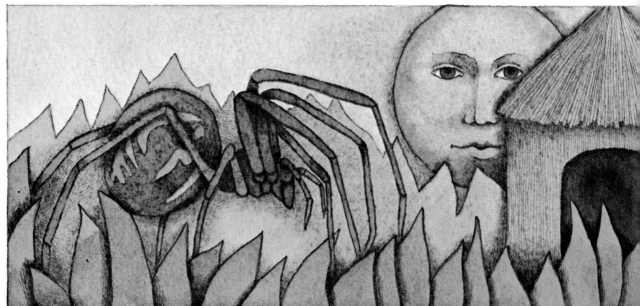

Well, the chief god wanted to put a stop to *that* silly idea. He said, "Very well, I'll grant you your wish. But you must do three things for me first. You must bring me a jar filled with live bees. Then I want a wild animal—a tiger. And last I want you to bring a big, long snake.

"Bring these to me," said the god, "and I will grant your wish." Of course, the god was sure that Anansi the spider could not do the three things.

Anansi cried, "Good. I will chase them down at once." And he started right away.

11

First Anansi took a clay jar and set out for a place where there were many bees. When he saw the bees, Anansi started to talk to himself.

"They will not be able to fly into this jar," he said. "Yes, they will; no, they won't! Yes, they will; no, they won't!"

The bees flew up and called, "What is wrong, Mr. Anansi?"

Anansi told them, "Some people say you cannot fly into this jar and fill it up."

"Of course we can! That's not hard," said the bees. So they did.

12

Then Anansi the spider shut the jar and took it to the chief god.

Next Anansi the spider had to catch a tiger and bring it to the chief god.

The following day Anansi took a large bag and went to a cave where a tiger lived. He got into the bag and sat down in front of the cave.

Then he shouted, "I'm sitting in a bag, I'm sitting in a bag! And now I can see the most beautiful sights!"

The tiger came running. It stared at the bag and listened to Anansi's shouts of joy. "Put me in the bag, Anansi," said the tiger. "I want to see the beautiful sights myself. Put me in the bag, too!"

Anansi got out of the bag and helped the tiger to get in. Then Anansi tied the bag closed. The tiger could not get out, and it could see nothing at all. There was nothing it could do to hurt Anansi. Anansi the spider pulled the bagged tiger away to the chief god's house.

The next day Anansi the spider went to find a large snake. He took with him a long plant stalk and some rope. When Anansi saw the snake, he called out, "Snake, my friend! Tiger says you are short. He says that you are even shorter than this long stalk. *I* say you are longer."

"Of course I am longer," said the snake, who was coiled around a tree. "If you want to be sure, I'll lie down beside the stalk and you can see." So the snake lay down beside the stalk.

14

"You're not straight enough," said Anansi. "You keep sliding back at one end or the other. I'm afraid that this is really a problem."

"What shall we do?" asked the snake.

"I know," said Anansi. "I can tie your head and tail to the stalk. That will keep you pulled out straight. Then I can really see how long you are."

"Do it," said the snake.

Soon the snake was tied to the stalk, tied from end to end. And Anansi pulled the snake along to the chief god's house.

The god was *very* surprised to get everything he had asked for. But he had to keep the promise to Anansi. So he said, "From now on, all stories in this land shall be owned by Anansi the Spider."

So they were. And you have just read one of them.

The Strongest Thing of All

Once there was a poor man. Each morning he went to the mountain. There he dug up stones. He broke them into pebbles with a large steel hammer. He carried the pebbles to the village, where he sold them.

Now the man thought that he was small and weak. Oh, how he wished and wished to feel great and strong.

One day he was standing on the mountain. The heat of the sun made him feel very hot and very weary.

"Oh," he said. "If I could be the sun, I would surely be happy. Nothing in the world is greater or stronger than the sun."

At once, just like that, he became the sun, burning high in the sky! He laughed when he saw people run indoors to hide from his rays. "Now I am the strongest of all things," said the man to himself.

Just then a cloud passed below. "Aha," cried the man. "I fear a cloud is stronger than the sun, for it can stop my rays. Oh, if I could only be a cloud. Then I would be the strongest thing."

Suddenly he became a cloud. "At last," he said, "I am the strongest." But then a wind came. It pushed the cloud up and carried it across the sky. The man saw that the cloud was not as strong as the wind.

"I must become the wind," thought the man. "The wind is the strongest thing of all." So he became the wind.

He played with the clouds, pushing them this way and that. He laughed to himself and said, "Oh, how fine it is to be the wind, the strongest thing of all." He blew and shook trees and houses. Then he blew at a mountain. But the mountain did not move, no matter how hard the wind blew.

"So," he thought, "the wind is weaker than the mountain. I wish to become a mountain."

And just as suddenly as before, he was a great mountain. The wind could not move him, and the man was happy.

Then he looked down and saw a poor man walking up the mountain. The poor man took stones from the mountain. With a steel hammer the man broke the stones into pebbles.

"Oh, I see at last!" the mountain roared. "People are the strongest, for they can break mountains. I want to be a person. Then I will be the strongest thing of all."

So the mountain became a man, as he had been at the start. He was still a poor man. But now he was a proud man, for he knew he was the strongest thing of all.

Atalanta's Race

They say that there was once a young woman by the name of Atalanta. You may believe her story or not, as you like — but it is a good old story all the same.

Atalanta loved to run, and oh, she was fast on her feet. She ran for the joy of it, racing with the wild things of the woods. It was said that she could move as swiftly as the birds in flight. Her father, the king, was very proud of her.

Now, Atalanta had no wish to marry. She answered "No" to all the young men who asked. "I am happy as I am," she said.

But the young men would not believe her, and they would not go away and let her be happy by herself.

At last Atalanta could think of only one thing to do. She said that anyone who wished to marry her must race against her. She would even give a head start. If any of them outran her, she would marry him.

But any young man who lost the race against her must die that very day. The king's officers would see to it.

Atalanta hoped in this way to be rid of all the young men. "Who would want to run such a race as that?" she thought.

And indeed, there were many young men who gave up the chase and went back to their homes. They were busy, they said. They suddenly remembered that they were needed at their homes.

But some of them stayed and raced against Atalanta. They *always* lost. Almost every day some unhappy young man had to die. The swiftest runner in the land could not outrun swift young Atalanta.

Then one day from a far-off place came a young man named Hippomenes. He was gentle and kind, and he was tall and good to look upon. Little by little Atalanta started to like him better than any of the other young men. She did not think she wanted to race against Hippomenes.

"You had better not run against me," she told Hippomenes. "I'm sure to win and that will be the end of you."

"We'll see about that," Hippomenes said. He smiled, for he had a secret.

Hippomenes had been to see a goddess who lived on top of a great mountain. He had asked for help, and the goddess had said yes. She had given Hippomenes three golden apples and told him what to do.

When all was ready for the race, Atalanta tried again to keep Hippomenes from running, for she liked him more and more. But he would not give up.

So the race started—and Hippomenes had the three golden apples with him.

Atalanta gave him a good head start and then chased swiftly after him. Hippomenes heard her coming close behind him. He knew she was about to pass him. Hippomenes took one of the golden apples from his shirt and threw it onto the ground behind him.

Now, young Atalanta had always admired beautiful things. She saw the golden apple shine in the sunlight. She saw how beautiful it was as it fell from Hippomenes' hand to the ground, and she stopped to pick it up.

Hippomenes ran very fast. But what of that? In no time at all, Atalanta was as close behind as before.

Then Hippomenes took the second apple from his shirt and threw it up into the air. It fell into some tall grass behind him. Once more Atalanta stopped and picked it up, for this second apple was more beautiful than the first.

It took her a long time to find the apple in
the tall grass. When she looked up again,
Hippomenes was far away. She whirled and ran
fast to catch up — but catch up she did.

She was about to pass, so Hippomenes threw
the last apple. This time he threw it far to one
side, where the ground ran down to a river.

Atalanta's quick eye saw that this apple was
far more beautiful than the other two.

Then suddenly she knew why Hippomenes threw the apples. He wanted to trick her and outrun her. But she would show him! She would get this last apple and win the race, too. She whirled and ran after the apple and picked it up. Then she turned again to the race. She saw that Hippomenes was almost at the row of trees that would end the race.

Atalanta ran like the wind, more swiftly than she had ever run before. And she caught up with Hippomenes just as he was about to win. Atalanta and Hippomenes tied in the race!

Atalanta was very hurt and angry because of Hippomenes' trick. And Hippomenes felt terrible when he saw Atalanta.

"I am truly sorry for what I did, Atalanta," said Hippomenes. "You are my good friend, and I admire you. I should not have tried to trick you in the race."

Just then the king came over to Atalanta.

"Well," he said to her. "Are you going to marry Hippomenes or not? It's up to you because the race was a tie."

Atalanta knew that Hippomenes was the nicest, kindest, gentlest young man she had ever met. And she could see that he was indeed sorry for what he had done.

"Yes," she said. "I am going to marry Hippomenes."

Hippomenes and Atalanta were married the very next day, and they were never sorry, for they lived in great joy together.

Photos by Leonard Kamsler, courtesy of
Ringling Bros. and Barnum & Bailey Circus.

The Daring Young Man

by DINA ANASTASIO

Every morning Tito Gaona puts on his
running shoes and runs three miles. Tito is not a
racer, but, like a racer, Tito is in training. He is
training for one of the hardest tricks
known—four back somersaults off a flying
trapeze.

There was a time when people thought that
no one would even be able to do three somersaults
from a flying trapeze. Only a few have ever
mastered this trick and some have died trying.
But Tito Gaona has done three somersaults in the
air many, many times.

30

Tito does the trick almost every day. The triple somersault has become so easy for Tito that he sometimes does it with his eyes closed.

If you have ever been to the circus, you may have seen Tito Gaona swinging on a trapeze high above your head. You may have seen him flying, turning, and spinning into the hands of a man on a second trapeze. This man is Tito's "catcher" and he is very important to Tito. The catcher must catch Tito's hands in just the right way and at just the right time. If the catcher does not, Tito might fall to the net below in such a way that he would hurt himself badly.

Photos by Leonard Kamsler, courtesy of Ringling Bros. and Barnum & Bailey Circus.

Tito is the king of the trapeze. Every night Tito climbs up, up, up, until he is standing on a platform high above the circus elephants, the dancing bears, and the beautiful white horses. He stands on the platform for a few seconds and waits, watching his catcher swinging upside down nearby. The circus band plays far below.

Photos by Leonard Kamsler, courtesy of Ringling Bros. and Barnum & Bailey Circus.

Photos by Leonard Kamsler, courtesy of
Ringling Bros. and Barnum & Bailey Circus.

When he is ready, Tito takes hold of the bar, steps off the platform, and swings up into the air, high above the people. He swings gently for a few seconds, watching the catcher. Then, still timing himself with his catcher, Tito swings faster and faster. The band and crowd far below grow quiet. Tito knows that he has to let go of the trapeze at just the right second. He swings. He waits . . . waits . . . now!

33

Tito lets the bar slide from his hands and pushes his legs higher and higher until they are above his head. He is turning, turning in the air . . . one, two, three somersaults!

Tito flies up into the air. He whirls three times and falls, his hands out. The catcher is there. He catches Tito's hands, and the two of them swing gently in the air. The crowd is no longer quiet. Tito swings high above the roaring people.

Tito has done another triple somersault; he has done the almost impossible trick from his flying trapeze once again.

No one has ever done four somersaults in the air. People feel that the triple somersault is nearly impossible; surely four somersaults *are* impossible. Tito does not believe that. He would like to be the first person ever to do the impossible trick.

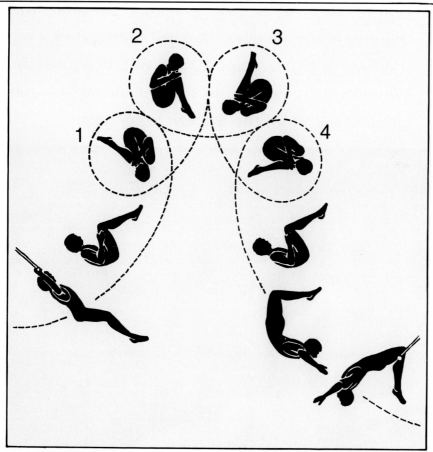

How Tito will do four somersaults in the air. He goes high into the air and whirls four times. As he comes out of the last somersault, he reaches for the hands of his catcher.

Tito has worked very hard for a long time to do this trick. He has come very close many times. He is able to do the four somersaults in the air, and sometimes he is able to touch the catcher's hands. But until now, the catcher and Tito have not been able to hold onto each other.

Everyone who watches Tito train can see how much he loves the trapeze. He sometimes even sings as he swings away from the platform. Tito believes that it is just a matter of time and training before he does the most daring trick ever tried on a flying trapeze. He will not give up. When he falls down into the net, he smiles and climbs back up to the trapeze to try again.

Photos by Leonard Kamsler, courtesy of
Ringling Bros. and Barnum & Bailey Circus.

Tito has been with the circus from the time
he was a boy. He has a sister who is a trapeze
artist. His great-grandfather, grandfather, and
father were all circus people. Tito has always
known that he would follow them.

Tito and his family live with the circus most of
the year. They move from city to city, doing one
or two shows every day. But there is always
enough time left over for Tito's dream.

Every night, after the show, Tito and his family work on the four somersaults. While Tito tries again, and again, and again, the others watch and help. They hope that maybe this will be the time that Tito's hands will lock with his catcher's hands. When the hands do not hold and Tito falls to the net, they say that it is all right, it will work the next time. Tito knows that some day his family will be right. He will do it. He climbs to the trapeze and tries the impossible trick one more time.

Tito's family is important to him. He knows that they will always be there, just as he knows

that his catcher will be there when he needs him. Photos by Leonard Kamsler, courtesy of Ringling Bros. and Barnum & Bailey Circus.
His family helps Tito feel strong and sure of himself. One day he will fly up into the air and whirl around in four somersaults. He will fall, and when his hands and the hands of his catcher lock, they will stay locked. One day the most impossible trick in the world will be done. It will be done because of many people—and one very brave and daring young man.

A Tale About Prefixes and Suffixes

In long ago times there were two villages named Prefix and Suffix. These villages were close by. But people kept to themselves and didn't bother with each other.

The people of Prefix were very clever. They discovered word parts such as *un*, *dis*, and *re*. They added these word parts to the beginnings of words. They made up many new words such as *unhappy*, *discover*, and *replay*.

The people of Suffix were also very, very clever. They discovered word parts such as *er*, *est*, and *ly*, which they added to the ends of words. They came up with new words such as *quicker*, *quickest*, and *quickly*.

40

One day some people from Prefix visited some people in Suffix. They began to teach each other about adding the beginning and ending word parts. How thrilled they were with all the new words they learned! They decided to go all around the country and teach word parts to everyone!

And that is how beginning and ending word parts came to be known as prefixes and suffixes.

Here is something that the people of Suffix taught the people of Prefix.

1. *er* means "more _____ than"
2. strong + er = stronger
3. *stronger* means "more *strong* than"

What do *louder* and *greater* mean?

If the suffix *est* means "the most," what does *strongest* mean? If *ly* means "in a way that is," what does *softly* mean? What does *slowly* mean?

The people of Prefix taught the Suffix people a few things, too.

1. *un* often means "not"
2. un + kind = unkind
3. *unkind* means "not kind"

What do *unhappy* and *unsure* mean?

If the prefix *dis* means "do not," what does *dislike* mean?

If *re* sometimes means "again," what does *reread* mean?

Look at the boldface words in the sentences below. Add the correct prefix *(un, dis, re)* or suffix *(er, est, ly)* to the word that is underlined so that it will have the same meaning as the boldface words.

1. The people of Prefix were not **more <u>smart</u>** than the people of Suffix.
2. Do you agree or **do** you **not <u>agree?</u>**
3. The **most <u>great</u>** day was when they became friends.
4. They learned **in a <u>quick</u> way** from each other.
5. **<u>Read</u> again** the story and decide if it is true or **not <u>true</u>**.

The Big Town

City Street

People rushing here and there,
Stores and buildings everywhere,
Traffic lights that STOP and GO,
Honks and beeps and horns that blow,
Pigeons finding crumbs to eat—
that's what makes a city street!

VIVIAN GOULED

44

City Spaces, City Places

What's Down There?

A big city is a busy place. It is crowded with people and traffic. Look up, and you can see tall buildings that seem to touch the sky. Stand on any street corner and you can hear, feel, and see the busy city all around you.

The city is a crowded place. Every bit of space counts—even the space under the ground. You cannot see what lies under the streets of a city. But if you could, you might be very surprised. Under the buildings and streets of a city are a lot of things that help to keep a city working. What's down there, under the street? Many, many things.

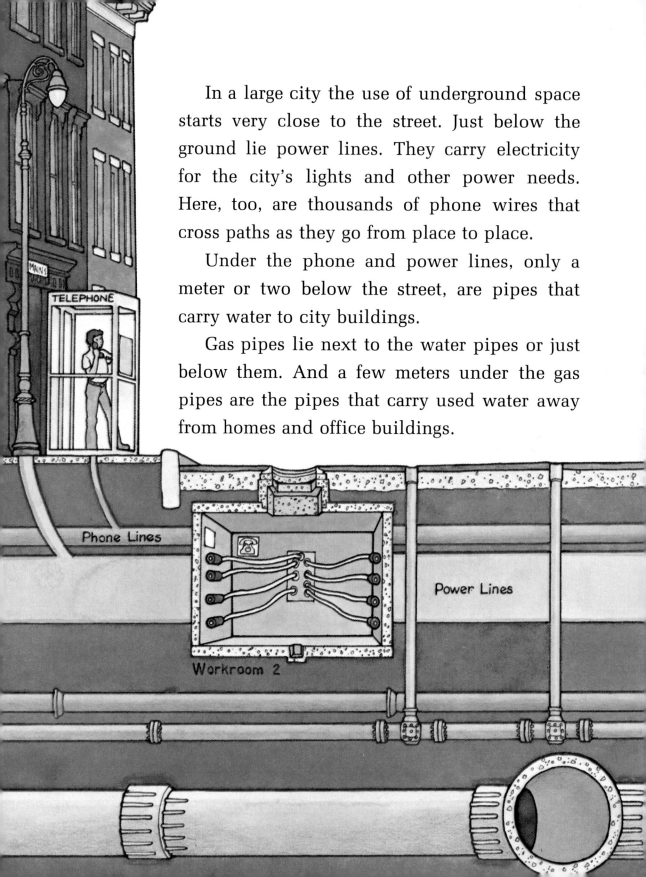

In a large city the use of underground space starts very close to the street. Just below the ground lie power lines. They carry electricity for the city's lights and other power needs. Here, too, are thousands of phone wires that cross paths as they go from place to place.

Under the phone and power lines, only a meter or two below the street, are pipes that carry water to city buildings.

Gas pipes lie next to the water pipes or just below them. And a few meters under the gas pipes are the pipes that carry used water away from homes and office buildings.

MAINS

TELEPHONE

Phone Lines

Workroom 2

Power Lines

But that's not all there is under the streets. There are also workroom spaces, where workers can fix breaks in pipes or power lines.

The pipes and lines under the city street are crowded very close together. There is sometimes hardly a bit of space left over. In some places there are so many things that not even a pencil can fit into the space left over.

Workroom 1

Water Pipe

Gas Pipe

Waste Water

47

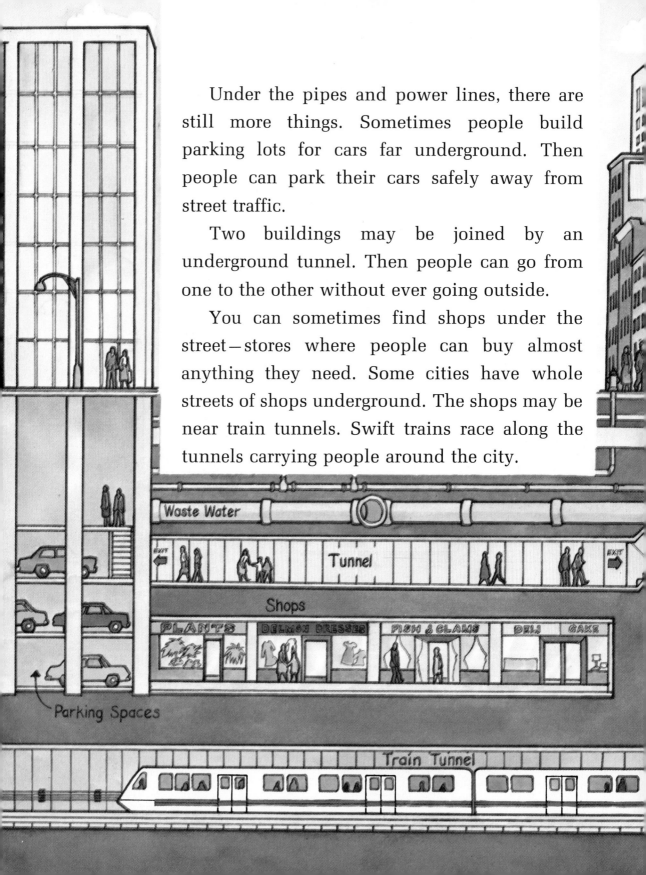

Under the pipes and power lines, there are still more things. Sometimes people build parking lots for cars far underground. Then people can park their cars safely away from street traffic.

Two buildings may be joined by an underground tunnel. Then people can go from one to the other without ever going outside.

You can sometimes find shops under the street—stores where people can buy almost anything they need. Some cities have whole streets of shops underground. The shops may be near train tunnels. Swift trains race along the tunnels carrying people around the city.

Waste Water

EXIT Tunnel EXIT

Shops

PLANTS DELMON DRESSES FISH & CLAMS DELI CAKE

Parking Spaces

Train Tunnel

Deepest of all are great underground pipes called aqueducts. They may lie as much as a hundred meters below the street. The aqueducts are giant tunnels made in the hard rock. They carry water to the city from the far-off places where it is stored.

In some cities tunnels sit upon tunnels, as many as four or five deep. And still, workers keep digging under the ground. They make room for more things—more pipes, wires, tunnels, and other things that the city needs.

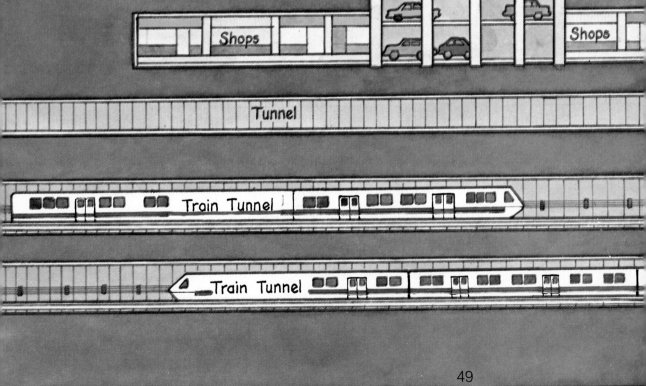

What's Up There?

A city uses much of the space below ground. It uses much of the space above it, too. The Green family lives on the forty-second story of a large city building. The building has more than two thousand rooms. The Greens live in five of the rooms.

Sometimes Mr. Green's daughter, Martha, goes to buy milk. Does Martha get in the elevator and go all the way down to the street? She does not. She goes to the milk machine near the elevator and puts her money in. Click, click, out comes the milk!

On top of the building is a playground. Martha and Pat can take the elevator to the highest floor and go out onto the roof. There they can play with their friends. They can even go swimming. Sometimes they look down at the other city buildings.

Each weekday morning Mr. and Mrs. Green go to work. How do they do that? They get into the elevator and go down to Floor 10. Then they get out, for the big office they work in all day is on that floor.

Sometimes the Green family goes out shopping—and they do not even leave the building! The first two floors of the building are filled with stores of many kinds: clothing stores, food stores, bookstores.

The Greens can also take a walk in a place that looks very much like a park. But it is not a park. It is the shopping space on the first floor. It has many trees and a big pool of water.

When it is cold or rainy out, the Greens do not worry. They can stay inside. And when it is very hot, they don't worry, for their building is nice and cool.

Do the Greens ever go out of their building? Of course they do. They go out to walk around the city. And the Greens have a car that is parked under the building. Sometimes they all jump into the car and ride to the cool, beautiful mountains.

The Greens like the trees and farms and spaces outside the city. But they also like their home in the city.

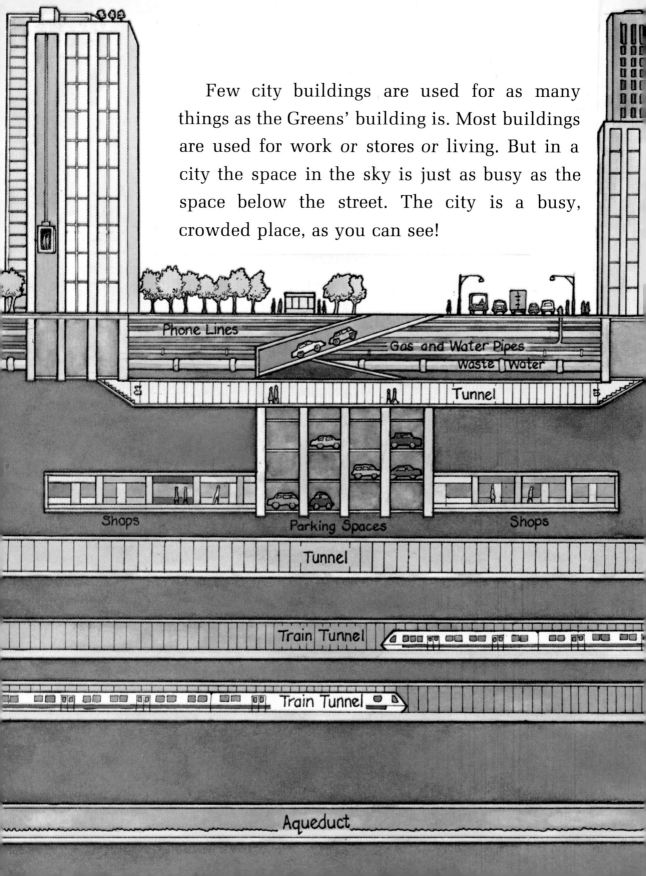

Few city buildings are used for as many things as the Greens' building is. Most buildings are used for work or stores or living. But in a city the space in the sky is just as busy as the space below the street. The city is a busy, crowded place, as you can see!

Phone Lines

Gas and Water Pipes

Waste Water

Tunnel

Shops

Parking Spaces

Shops

Tunnel

Train Tunnel

Train Tunnel

Aqueduct

The Person Downstairs
A MUSICAL PLAY

Time: Not long ago

Place: The home of the Andrews family,
on the top floor of a city building

People in the play:

Ray Andrews, 10

Linda Andrews, 8

Chet Andrews, 6

Mrs. Andrews

Mr. Andrews

The Woman Downstairs

Carla Lopez

55

Act I Scene One

(It is a rainy summer day. Ray and Chet are playing inside with a toy car and a fire truck. Linda is bouncing a ball.)

CHET: Look out, here I come! Clang, clang, here comes the fire truck!

RAY: Crash! I ran right into you!

LINDA: Shhhh, you two, or you'll wake up the man downstairs.

CHET: Who cares? He shouldn't be sleeping in the daytime.

RAY: Linda is right. He works at night, so he has to sleep during the day.

CHET: I wish he would get another job, a day job.

LINDA: I wish that he and his wife would move so we could make noise again. We used to have much more fun when the Caspers lived downstairs.

RAY: Yes, I sure miss Tommy and Jill. Now we're the only children in the building. If only those new people downstairs had some children, we could go to the roof and play with them.

CHET: No we couldn't. It's raining, so we're stuck in here. R-r-r-r-r-r-r!

(Chet pushes his fire truck.)

RAY: Look out, fire truck—CRASH!

(There is a knock at the door.)

LINDA: I'll get the door.

(She does that and a woman comes in.)

WOMAN: Please, children, don't make so much noise; my husband needs his sleep.

RAY: We're sorry. We'll try to be quieter.

WOMAN: Thank you, dear, I knew you would understand.

(The woman goes out.)

LINDA: Quiet, quiet, what a bore!

(Linda, then Ray, then Chet sing the round.)

Quiet, quiet,
Quiet, quiet . . .
What a bore,
What a bore!
Why can't we be noisy,
Why can't we be noisy,
Like before,
Like before?

Scene Two

(It is late afternoon of the next day. Dad comes in from work.)

DAD: Hello, everyone.

MOM, RAY, LINDA, CHET: Hello!

DAD: I just ran into the woman from downstairs.

LINDA: Did you hurt her?

DAD: Not really. She told me some news.

RAY: Is her husband getting a day job?

DAD: No, but he got a job with a company in a different city, and the family is going to move away in two weeks.

LINDA, RAY, CHET: Hurray!

CHET: Then we can make lots and lots of noise.

MOM: I think you'll be able to make *some* noise, Chet. But no one who lives downstairs will be able to live with *lots* of noise.

LINDA: The Caspers did! They made as much noise as we do.

DAD: Well, they were different.

RAY: They sure were.

MOM: Do you remember the times we and the Caspers sang together?

DAD: Well, we can sing now. We'll sing about being as quiet as mice. Children, you will be the mice.

(Mom and Dad stand side by side as Linda, Ray, and Chet crawl to them. All sing.)

MOM and DAD: You'll be mice,
You'll be mice,

CHILDREN: *We'll* crawl and creep,
Let them all sleep.

ALL: We'll never make any sound
at all,
Unless we happen to jump
and fall,
And knock the pictures right
off the wall—
Won't that be nice!

Scene Three

(It is a morning three weeks later. Chet and Linda are playing, and Ray is standing by the window.)

RAY: Come here, look outside, you two! There's a big truck in front of our building, and some people are taking out chairs and things. Somebody is moving in.

(Chet and Linda run to the window.)

LINDA: It must be the people who are going to live downstairs. Hurray!

CHET and RAY: Hurray!

(Mom runs into the room.)

MOM: Shhhh, children, the people downstairs will hear you.

LINDA: You don't have to say that any more, because they have left and the new people are moving in.

CHET: Do you think these people have any children? I don't see any toys.

RAY: Then we'd better make all the noise we can right now.

LINDA and CHET: Right!

(They all dance and sing.)

ALL: Sing, yell, hammer, scream,
Loud as we know how,
Noisily, noisily, noisily, noisily,
We can holler now!

RAY: Wait! Stop singing and come look! There's a big set of drums down there. They *must* have some children.

LINDA: And if their children play the drums, they won't even hear it when we make noise.

ALL: Hurray for the people downstairs!

End of Act 1

Act 2 Scene One

(It is the next night and Dad comes home from work. A woman is with him.)

DAD: Everyone, come and meet Ms. Carla Lopez. Yesterday she moved in downstairs. She just moved to our city.

MOM: We're very glad to meet you, Ms. Lopez.

CARLA: Please call me Carla.

RAY: Hello. Where are your children?

LINDA: Yes, and how old are they?

CHET: How many children do you have?

CARLA: Just a second! I haven't any children. Why do you think I do?

CHET: We saw those big drums yesterday. If you don't have children, who owns the drums?

CARLA: They're mine.

LINDA, RAY, CHET: They're yours?

CARLA: That's right. I use them for my work. I play the drums in a band, so every day I play them at home for a while.

LINDA: Do you make lots of noise?

CARLA: Well, I try not to bother anyone, but I do make a lot of noise. I hope I won't bother you too much.

MOM: You won't bother us at all.

DAD: Carla, you go and make all the noise you want. Then my children can make all the noise they want, and everyone will be happy.

CARLA: Great! Well, I had better be going. It was very nice to meet all of you. I'm sure I'll see you again soon.

DAD, MOM, LINDA, RAY: Good night. It was nice meeting you!

CHET: See you soon!

(Carla goes out.)

LINDA: So she plays the drums!

RAY: She'll never hear us. We can make noise all day long.

CHET: Tomorrow, when we come home from school, we'll shout and yell.

(The children sing.)

Tomorrow we will yell,
Tomorrow we will yell—
We'll yell and shout
When school gets out—
Tomorrow we will yell!

Scene Two

(It is five days later. Loud drumming is heard from the room downstairs.)

RAY *(shouting)*: She's playing those drums louder and louder, and it hurts my head.

LINDA *(shouting)*: Well, she's not playing as loud as she did yesterday.

MOM *(shouting)*: I can't hear you.

CHET: Mom, I want to watch TV.

MOM: All right.

CHET: But I won't be able to hear what's happening, Mom.

MOM *(laughing)*: Well, you said you wanted to *watch* it. You didn't say you wanted to *listen* to it, too.

CHET *(laughing)*: Oh, Mom.

MOM: Come on, let's all sing so we won't be able to hear the drumming.

ALL: The drummer's new in town,
The drummer's new in town,
She'll drum and play,
And crash all day—
We wish she'd quiet down.

Scene Three

(It is night, a week later.)

LINDA: She's quiet at last!

RAY: For the first time in weeks, it seems.

MOM: That's true.

(There is a knock at the door.)

CHET *(opening the door)*: It's Carla.

MOM: Please come in, Carla.

CARLA: I just wanted to say hello and see how everyone is.

DAD: We're very glad you stopped by. Here, sit down, Carla; there's something we want to talk to you about.

CARLA (*sitting*): I *thought* there was something you wanted to tell me.

MOM: Why did you think so?

CARLA: Well, I saw Chet playing downstairs today, and I said hello. But he wouldn't even talk to me.

MOM: Chet!

DAD (*to Carla*): Chet hasn't been himself lately.

CHET: Yes, because of all the drum noise.

DAD: Chet!

CARLA (*laughing*): Oh, that's all right. That's what I thought it was, and that's why I came up here. I wanted to know when I could play without bothering you. The people who live below me are not home from 2 until 4:30 in the afternoon. Is it all right if I play then?

LINDA: Sure, we get home from school at 3:30.

RAY: Then we can make lots of noise while you play the drums.

CHET: Then it will be quiet when I want to watch the TV.

RAY and LINDA: And when we have to study.

MOM: And when I want to read.

DAD: I think your drumming from 2 until 4:30 is fine with everyone.

CARLA (*smiling*): Noise and quiet at last!

(They all sing.)

DAD (*to children*): Some noise time for you,

CARLA: Some drum time for me,

ALL: Some quiet time for everyone,
    Better neighbors we'll be!
    Hurray for the person downstairs!

The End

"Reading" Pictures for Information

You can learn from some pictures just by looking at them. But, there are some pictures that you must both look at and *read*.

Look at this picture and read the words.

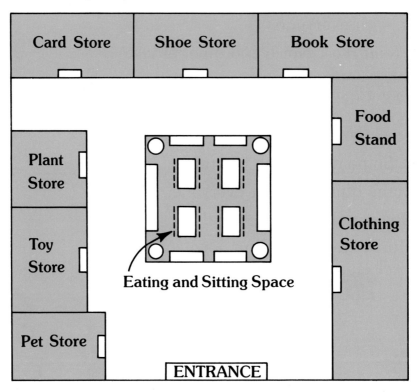

The picture is very helpful to people who are shopping. Pictures *can* give you a lot of information. When you study them you can quickly learn many new things.

Pictures like this are called *diagrams*. This diagram shows where the main parts of the shopping space are located.

Look at the diagram and answer these questions.

1. As you go into the shopping space, which store is on your left? Which store is on your right?
2. The shoe store is between the _____ store and the _____ store.
3. What is in the center of the shopping space?

A *bar graph* is another kind of diagram. The bar graph below gives information about telephones and cities. Did you know that Honolulu has more telephones than Kansas City? The bar graph shows that fact and other facts as well.

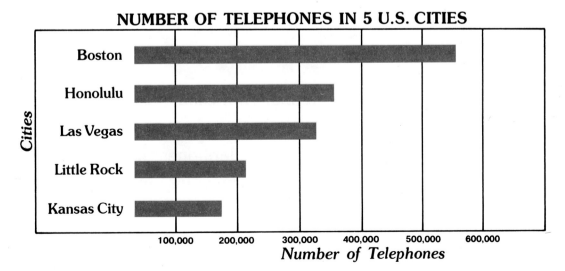

NUMBER OF TELEPHONES IN 5 U.S. CITIES

Bar graphs show how things are alike and how they are different. They *compare* things. The title of a graph tells what it is comparing. What can you learn from the title of the graph on page 73?

Read the names down the side of the graph. These are the cities that are being compared. Other graphs may compare people, animals, jobs, or many other things.

Look at the label at the bottom. It tells what the graph is measuring. What is this graph measuring?

Each colored bar stands for the number of telephones in one of the cities. Move your finger across a bar from left to right. When you come to the end of the bar, move your finger straight down to the number line. That will tell you the number of telephones in each city. How many telephones does each city have?

Use the bar graph to answer each question.
1. Which city has the most telephones?
2. Which city has more telephones than
   Little Rock, but fewer than Honolulu?
3. Which city has the fewest telephones?

Messages

Primer Lesson

Look out how you use proud words.
When you let proud words go, it is not
    easy to call them back.
They wear long boots, hard boots;
    they walk off proud; they can't
    hear you calling —
Look out how you use proud words.

CARL SANDBURG

76

A Letter in a Bottle

by EMILY RHOADS JOHNSON

Have you ever sent a letter by "bottle mail"?
If you have, you may never get an answer to it.
It may be that no one will ever get the message
that you put into the bottle.

"Bottle mail" is a very old way of sending
messages by sea. The message is put into a
bottle or into anything that floats. Then it is
thrown into the sea. It floats out of sight, carried
by the waves. It may or may not be found.

If that is so, why would a person want to send a letter this way? Well, it is surely great fun when someone *does* find the letter and sends an answer to it!

A few years ago a girl named Roberta was aboard a ship on the ocean. From there she sent a message by bottle. In her message Roberta told who she was and where she lived. She even told just where the ship was on the day she wrote the message.

When she finished writing, Roberta rolled up the paper and put it into a bottle. She closed the top and threw the bottle into the ocean.

A little more than a year later, Roberta got a letter. It was from a man who lived far away. He had seen Roberta's bottle on the beach, opened it up, and found the message inside.

Now Roberta and her friend hope to meet each other some day. They write to each other a lot. But they put their letters in mailboxes. Mailboxes are much surer than bottles when you have a message to send.

People started to use bottle mail hundreds of years ago. In 1493 Christopher Columbus did. He was aboard his ship, headed back to Spain from the New World. He was afraid that the ship might not get all the way back to Spain and that no one would ever hear of his great news.

So Columbus wrote down all that he wanted the world to know about the New World. He put his message into a box that would float and threw it into the water.

The box was found over 300 years later near Spain. Unfortunately, the precious documents were lost again, never to be found.

Why did Roberta's message take only a year, while Columbus's message took so long? The answer is ocean currents.

An ocean current is like a river that runs in the ocean. There are many currents. Some move fast, and some move slowly. They move in different ways.

Even if two bottles are thrown into the ocean at the same time, no one can tell what will happen to them. Each one might be caught by different currents and move in different paths.

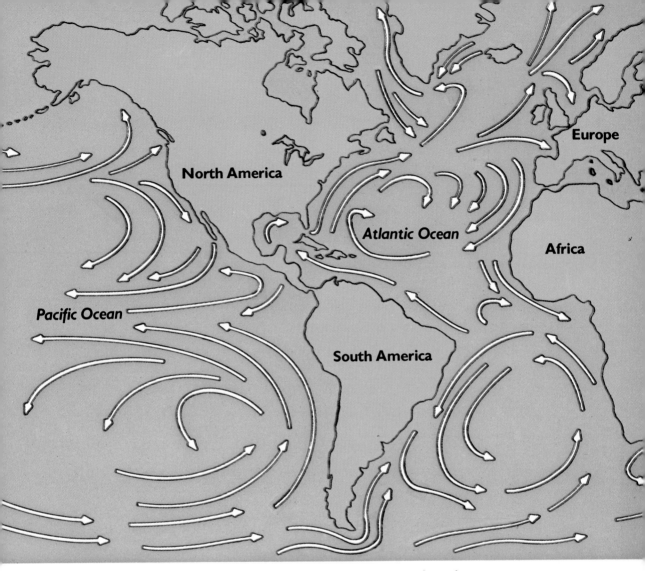

Ocean currents of the Atlantic and Pacific Oceans. The arrows show the paths a bottle may take when it is tossed into the ocean.

One bottle may float in a swift current. The other may move in a very slow one. One bottle may go thousands of kilometers in a year. The other may float far from land for hundreds and hundreds of years.

If you are ever on a boat in the ocean and want to send a message by bottle, here are a few things to remember.

1. Use a good bottle. Put clean, dry sand in it to make it stay straight up as it floats.

2. Don't forget to write your name and where you live in your message. If you like, put a penny or some small thing in the bottle along with your message.

3. Put a good stopper, like a cork, in the top of your bottle. Make sure that the stopper is tight enough to keep water out of the bottle. Stick something colorful into the stopper. Then your bottle can be seen better.

4. Throw the bottle as far as you can.

Then—wait. Maybe someday—just maybe—someone will answer your message sent by bottle mail.

The Secret Three

by MILDRED MYRICK

"What's this?" Billy said. He bent over to pick up a green bottle that was lying on the beach. He had to dig it up. It wasn't easy, for it was weighted down with wet sand sticking to it.

"Look, Mark!" Billy said. "There's writing on a piece of paper inside this bottle."

83

Billy took the paper out of the bottle. "I think it's a message, but I can't read it," he said.

Surprised, Billy's friend Mark looked at the paper. But Mark could not read the writing.

This is what they saw:

I live on the island. I would like to know some of my neighbors. It would be nice to have a club with some boys or girls who can read this writing.

Tom

The two boys took the bottle and the paper up the beach to Billy's house, where Mark was staying for the rest of the summer. They held the paper upside down and they held it right side up, but they could not read the writing.

Suddenly Billy caught sight of the paper in a mirror on the wall. "Mark! Look in the mirror!" he cried. "Now we can read the writing."

This is what they read:

I live on the island. I would like to know some of my neighbors. It would be nice to have a club with some boys or girls who can read this writing.
Tom

"Isn't this great?" Billy said. "Clubs are lots of fun."

"Yes. We can send secret messages to each other," Mark said.

"We could have a name for our club," said Billy. "Let's see, there are three of us. THE SECRET THREE!"

"That's a good name," Mark said. "I hope Tom likes it."

The boys ran along the shore to find Billy's dad and show him the message.

"The new lighthouse keeper over on the island has a boy," Billy's dad said. "Maybe this message is from him."

The boys looked across the grey water at the lighthouse. "Will Tom get a message if we send one in a bottle?" asked Billy.

"You can try it," said his father. "This bottle came in with the high tide, when the ocean came far up on the beach. Maybe the next tide will take it back."

"When's the next tide?" asked Mark.

"Take a look in the newspaper," said Billy's father. And they did.

The paper showed that the tide had been high on their beach a little after seven that morning and would be high again late that day, shortly before eight.

Then the boys worked on a secret message to send to Tom. Mark knew a good way to do it. He said, "We write down the alphabet, and then we give each letter a number, see?"

Here is the secret alphabet and the message the boys wrote:

a	b	c	d	e	f	g	h	i	j	k	l	m
1	2	3	4	5	6	7	8	9	10	11	12	13

n	o	p	q	r	s	t	u	v	w	x	y	z
14	15	16	17	18	19	20	21	22	23	24	25	26

Two 2·15·25·19 found your message. We know your name is 20·15·13· Can you tell us our names ? Do you think THE 19·5·3·18·5·20 THREE is a 7·15·15·4 name for a 3·12·21·2 ?

13·1·18·11 and 2·9·12·12·25

The boys put the message in the bottle and took the bottle to the beach. They were just in time. The tide was starting to go out, away from the shore. When they could not see the bottle, Billy and Mark went home.

The next high tide came at a little after six the next morning. Mark and Billy were on the beach soon after that, but they didn't find the bottle.

"We can look after the next high tide," said Mark. "Maybe Tom didn't find the bottle last night. Maybe he's finding it right now!"

After supper that day, they went back to the beach, and Billy carried a little mirror with him. They walked a long time, on and on along the shore, but they did not find the bottle.

Then as Billy stopped to pick up a shell, Mark spotted something green on the beach.

"Here it is!" he cried. "And there's a paper inside it!"

Billy came running. Together, the two boys read the message with the help of Billy's little mirror.

Your names are Mark and Billy. I had a hard time with your message. THE SECRET THREE can meet here tomorrow. Please come with the fisherman.
Tom.

"Great," said Mark, "but, Billy, who's the fisherman?"

"I know him," said Billy. "He's a neighbor of ours. Let's go look for him."

They found the fisherman at home, and he listened with a smile to the story the boys had to tell. "Sounds like a good club," he said. "I'll take you to the island if you ask your father first."

Later, Billy and Mark sat on the beach, talking.

"When we get to the island, how will we know which boy is Tom?" Mark asked.

"We could have a secret sign," Billy said. "When a boy holds up his hand and makes the sign, we'll know he's Tom."

The boys sent Tom this message:

Dear 20·15·13,
    Here is our secret 19·9·7·14. When we see you we will hold up 19·9·24 fingers — that stands for the number of letters in secret. You have to hold up 20·8·18·5·5 fingers — that stands for the number of boys in the 3·12·21·2. We give the 19·9·7·14 when we meet.
      2·9·12·12·25 and 13·1·18·11.

The next day, Billy and Mark got ready to go to the island. "Better take a lightweight coat, boys," Billy's father told them. "The air can be a lot colder on the island, you know."

The boys could hardly sit still as the fisherman pushed off from the shore. They liked the ride in the boat.

"There's a boy waiting," Mark said as the little fishing boat neared the island. "Maybe it's Tom."

"We'd better be sure," Billy said. "We'll give the secret sign."

As the boy onshore ran to meet them, Billy and Mark held up six fingers. The boy held up three fingers. Mark gave a shout.

They knew the boy was Tom!

That day, THE SECRET THREE held its first meeting.

The artist Willem de Kooning at work in his studio. Hans Namuth

Looking at Paintings

Most people use words to send messages. But artists use colors, lines, and shapes. Paintings show what artists think and feel about things.

Artists have painted pictures of almost anything you can think of. They have painted circuses, busy cities, dark clouds, quiet ponds, and pools of water. They have painted young lambs in the grass, and even bulldozers and machines.

Look at the pictures on the following pages and see if you can tell what the artists tried to say in their paintings.

On these pages are two pictures of farms. In this one the artist used dark quiet colors to show the farm in late autumn. Look at the trees' limbs and the brown grass. What sort of feeling does the painting give you?

Evening at Kuerners, by Andrew Wyeth

The Old Oaken Bucket, by Grandma Moses

This artist painted what she had seen when she was a young girl. Her works of art help people feel what farms were like many years ago.

Would you call this painting sad or cheerful? Is the feeling of this painting different from that of the other farm painting? Can you say why?

Some painters paint pictures that look very real, while others try new ways of showing things.

Amateur Musicians, by Winslow Homer

Three Musicians, by Pablo Picasso
Oil on canvas; 6'7" x 7'3¾"

Look at the picture on the left and then
the one above. Which one looks more real?
Which one seems to be more playful? Do
you like one picture more than the other?
Can you say why?

Mrs. Mayer and Daughter, by Ammi Phillips

Here are two paintings, each showing a mother with her child — but how different they are in color, shape, and line! What kind of feeling does each picture give you? What do you think each artist was trying to say?

100

Mother and Child, by Mary Cassatt

Hunters in the Snow, by Pieter Bruegel the Elder

Without words artists can give messages to us. Look at all the paintings again and pick out the one you like the best. See if you can find something in it you did not see before. Try to understand what the artists felt as they painted; look, and let the artists speak to you!

Getting the Message

Here is a secret message that is like the ones in "The Secret Three." Can you work out what it says? Do 25–15–21 know 23–8–1–20 a 3–15–4–5 is?

If your answer is 25–5–19 or YES, tell the class what a *code* is.

Codes have been used for a long time to send messages. Some codes use numbers. Others may use letters.

Look at the picture of the girl. Her name is Sarah. She is on a treasure hunt and has just picked up her first clue. The clue is written in a code that used letters. Read every other letter in each word. Can you figure out what it says?

L–M–O–Q–O–T–K–U   U–V–N–S–D–P–E–T–R
T–A–H–B–E   B–N–I–C–G   O–D–A–G–K   T–J–R–L–E–M–E.

Did you "decode" the message?

You may not think about it, but each time you read, you are "decoding" words. When you work out the sounds that letters stand for, you can read the words and get the message.

Now let's get back to Sarah and her treasure hunt. You will need your decoding skills to work out an important word in each clue.

Sarah found this clue under the oak tree:

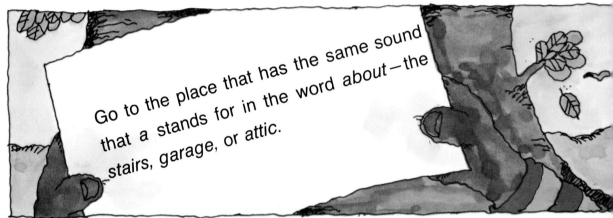

Go to the place that has the same sound that a stands for in the word about—the stairs, garage, or attic.

After Sarah got to the right place, she picked up this clue:

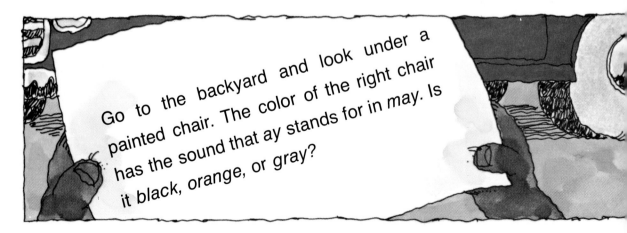

Go to the backyard and look under a painted chair. The color of the right chair has the sound that ay stands for in may. Is it black, orange, or gray?

Which chair should Sarah look under?

Sarah looked under the right chair and found this clue:

Go to the front yard. Look under the thing that has the same sound as the *u* in *bugs.* Things in the yard are *bucket, bugle,* and *boot.*

Sarah looked under the bugle, but the clue was not there. Where should she have looked?

Sarah soon understood her mistake. Then she looked under the right thing and found the clue. This is what it said:

This is the last clue. You will find your treasure in the living room. It will be on top of something that has the same sound that *ay* stands for in *stay*—a *lamp, chair,* or *table.*

Where should Sarah look to find her treasure?

Turn the page to find out what Sarah's treasure was.

TRY THIS

1. Write or tell the answer to each question.

   a. Sarah's treasure was a puppy. Does the u in *puppy* stand for the same sound as the u in *cute, fur,* or *bus*?

   b. Pretend you want to hide a clue. You hide it in something whose name has the sound that *oo* stands for in *good*. Would you hide it in a *boot* or a *book*?

   c. If you were told to go to a place that had the sound that *o* stands for in *hop,* would you go to the *store,* the *pond,* or *home*?

2. Write a secret message and give it to a friend. Use one of the codes on page 103 or make up your own code. If your friend can't work out your code, give a clue!

106

Animal World

THE ELEPHANT'S NOSE

A baby elephant's nose,
If you please,
Only reaches
His knees,
But he always
Always knows
When he's grown up
Because his nose
Has grown down
To reach his toes.

LAURA ARLON

108

OOKIE, THE WALRUS

by WILLIAM BRIDGES

Ookie was the only walrus at the marine zoo. That was part of the trouble.

She liked people a lot. But the zoo keepers and the people who came to see Ookie couldn't be with her all the time. That was another part of the trouble. Ookie was just about the most playful walrus that marine zoo had ever known. That was the biggest part of the trouble.

Oh, yes! That young walrus, without meaning to, made a lot of trouble one summer at the marine zoo.

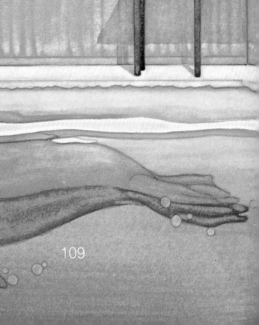

You see, Ookie had her own salt-water pool at
the zoo. And there was another salt-water pool
very near hers where two little seals lived. Ookie
could see the little seals. They raced after each
other in the water, swimming, rolling, playing in
all kinds of ways.

But there was a wall about a meter high
between the two pools. At first Ookie would just
stand up on her back flippers, look over the wall,
and watch the actions of the seals. Then one day
she decided she was going to play with them.

One of the zoo keepers was eating his lunch not far from the pools. Suddenly he heard the people around the seals' pool. They were laughing and shouting. He ran to the pool to see what had happened.

Oh, no!

There was Ookie in the seals' pool, trying to catch the little seals. Of course the seals didn't know what this big animal was. They hadn't been able to look over *their* wall and see Ookie. They were scared! Maybe they thought Ookie wanted to eat them. But she only wanted to play.

"I thought I would *die*," the keeper said later. "I guess I was almost as scared as the seals were. Ookie might have hurt them without meaning to. Or, if she'd caught up with them and they'd bitten her, she could have been hurt herself."

The keeper quickly called some other people. They pulled open the gate that was between Ookie's pool and the seals' pool. Then they pushed her and pulled her, and pushed and pulled, until they got her back home. Good! They shut the gate and went away.

Do you think that that took care of the matter? Oh, no!

Ookie was back in the seals' pool before the people had time to bat an eye or say, "Ookie the Walrus." So again they pushed her back home. But no sooner had they turned to go than she was back in the seals' pool again. And again.

"She's climbing the wall!" the keepers cried. Indeed she was. She was having so much fun she could have played this game all night.

At last some of the keepers went to Ookie's pool and spied on her. They sat in back and watched her, making sure she couldn't see them. They *had* to know how she did it.

First she got up on tiptoe, using her back flippers like feet. Then she put her front flippers over the top of the wall. Next she put her back flippers into a little space above the floor. Then with a pulling motion, she used her front flippers to get herself up onto the wall.

Once Ookie was on top of the wall, she just rolled off, and there she was, in the seals' pool. The fall didn't hurt her a bit.

Well, the zoo keepers knew they'd better do something and do it pretty quickly.

They decided that they would need a really high wall to keep Ookie in her own pool. Oh, yes! A higher wall would end the problem!

So they made the wall higher.

Ookie climbed over it.

They made the wall higher still.

Ookie climbed over it.

The zoo spent a lot of time and a lot of money building and adding to that wall. They made it higher, higher, higher. And Ookie still climbed over it. She had never had so much fun.

The keepers were worried, though. They were afraid that Ookie would hurt herself now, rolling off that high wall.

But Ookie knew when to stop. That was easy—she stopped when the wall got to be too high for her. She stopped when it was almost three meters high and she couldn't see over it or climb to the top, no matter how hard she tried.

Guess what. The zoo keepers started to feel sorry for her then. "Poor thing! She needs to

play," they said. "Maybe she'd like a toy." So they
gave her a big, light ball to play with.

There were lots of things Ookie could do with
that ball. What she liked best was to lie floating
on her back, holding the big, round ball on her
big, round stomach with her flippers. That was
almost as much fun as playing with those little
seals. Or climbing over walls.

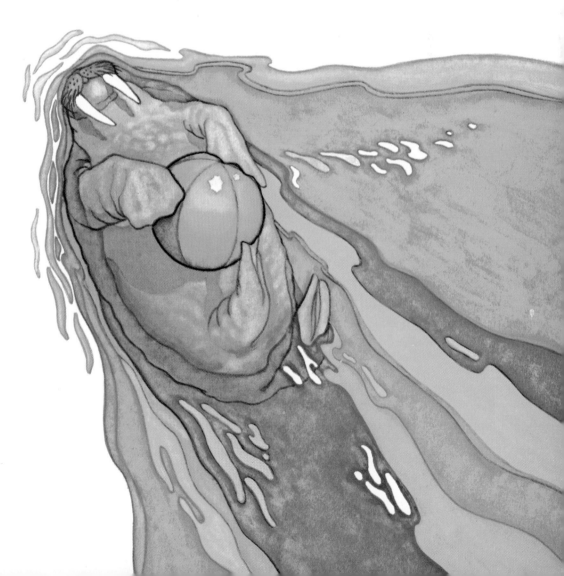

Finally, later that summer, something happened that really made Ookie happy. The seals were bigger. The keepers knew they wouldn't be afraid of Ookie anymore. So they opened the gate between the two salt pools.

Hurray! Ookie lost no time. She raced into the other pool. She didn't try to catch the seals this time. She just floated on her back and looked very happy.

Soon one of the seals swam over to Ookie and crawled onto her stomach. Ookie didn't care at all. Oh, no!

What could be better than a new friend?

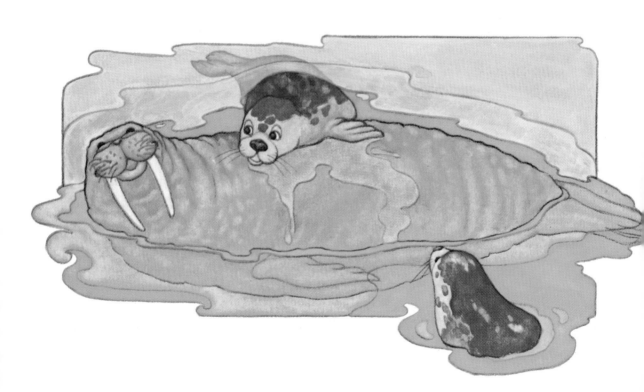

Dulary

by MORRIS WEEKS, JR.

There was a new face at the Philadelphia Zoo on a morning late in May.

It was a nice face. It was wide at the top, with a little hair and a long gray ear at each side. The face narrowed at the bottom to a long trunk. Above the trunk a pair of brown eyes looked out.

A face like this could only be an elephant's. This was a little girl elephant—really just a baby. She had an Indian name, Dulary (dōo·lä′·rē), which means "toy." Not even a year old, she was only a meter high, not much bigger than a big dog. Her weight, 120 kilograms, sounds like a lot for a baby—but in time she would grow to thousands of kilograms.

Record of Growth— Baby Elephant Dulary

	Date	Weight in Kilograms		
		Increase	Decrease	
Arrived	May 26			120
	June 2	20		140
	June 9	20		160
	June 16		3	157
	June 23			157
	June 30	7		164
	July 6		7	157
	July 19	7		164
	July 28	2		166
	August 4	1		167
	August 11	11		178
	August 18			

On that first morning at the Philadelphia Zoo, Dulary looked little and lost. She was in her own pen in the Children's Zoo with a woman named Ann Lewis. Ann had to help Dulary get used to a new home far from where she had lived.

What Dulary really needed was her mother. In the wild, little elephants do not leave their mothers until they are two years old or older.

So Ann Lewis did her best to play mother to little Dulary. She petted Dulary a lot and talked to her. She let Dulary feel her hands, legs, and face with the end of her trunk. Ann even put her hand in Dulary's wet red mouth and let her pull softly on it.

The zoo gates opened for the day. A crowd of children spied Dulary. Shouts and squeals and screams of joy filled the air. Children came running to make friends with the baby elephant. With "oh's" and happy shrieks, they crowded close to the wire fence around Dulary's pen. Of course they tried to pet her. And of course they gave her many of the nuts they had brought to give to the squirrels.

Dulary loved it. She ran around the pen calling softly. She pushed up to the fence, which was taller than she was. She put her trunk over the wire for nuts. It looked to the children as if she were smiling.

Ann watched Dulary and the children closely. She wanted to make sure that Dulary didn't hurt anyone by taking hold of a hand. And she had to make sure that the children didn't give Dulary anything to eat that might hurt her.

By the end of the day, the zoo knew that it had a new star. Everyone was talking about Dulary. The papers ran stories about her, with pictures. People said, "That new elephant sounds great. Let's go to the zoo and see her."

Mother to an Elephant

"I liked Dulary from the first day," Ann Lewis says, "and she liked me. She needed me. She counted on me to give her so many things—food, a little petting, a lot of care. She just knew I would give them to her. I worked hard at being a mother to her and at teaching her things she needed to know. You could tell she was very thankful.

"I came in every morning and fixed her food for the day. As soon as she saw me, her ears stood out, and she started to call. Then she walked up to me like a pet dog.

"And eat! She put on a lot of weight the first

few days. Then for a brief time, she lost some weight, so we gave her different food."

Dulary's new food was full of all sorts of good things. It even had bananas in it. With food like that, any animal would put on a few kilograms.

Four times a day, all summer long, Dulary got this food. It did the trick. By the time fall came, her weight was up to 225 kilograms. She was growing the way she should.

The children who came to see her loved to watch Dulary eat. Her trunk took up the food and blew it into her mouth. Of course, as soon as she had finished all that the zoo gave her, she was ready for more nuts.

Each afternoon Ann took Dulary for a walk around the winding streets of the zoo. Ann carried a stick to keep Dulary in line. But she never had to use it. Dulary loved Ann as a mother and would go anywhere Ann went. She waited for her walk just as she waited for Ann each morning, and she never tried to break away from her.

Only once did the zoo have any trouble with Dulary—and that was on Ann's day off.

That day two keepers from the Children's Zoo decided to take Dulary for her walk. She liked them, but she wasn't used to being with them, so she decided to set off on her own.

Suddenly Dulary started to run. One keeper lost his hold on her. Then she ran into the shrubs, and the other keeper lost sight of her, too. The cries of those keepers did not matter a bit to Dulary. She was happy as could be! But finally the two keepers did catch Dulary.

When she was not out walking, Dulary was
happy in her pen. Like many elephants, she
liked water, so a small pool was made for her.
She really made use of her pool on hot days.
Ann took off her shoes and went in, too.

"Dulary just loved to be with someone," Ann
says. "Why, if I sat down in her pen to rest, she
might walk over and stand very close to me. I
think she would have sat on my *lap* if I'd let
her. Think of that — a lap elephant!"

Growing Up

Time passed. Thousands of boys and girls and nearly as many grown-ups had come to see Dulary that first summer of her life. She spent her first winter indoors with the other animals. Then there was another summer as the star of the Children's Zoo, with Ann as her keeper. In the meantime Dulary grew and grew and grew.

By the end of her second winter in the zoo, she was too big for the Children's Zoo. She was far from grown-up, and she was as friendly as ever. But she just didn't fit in with baby ducks and baby lions anymore. The zoo decided that Dulary would go to the Elephant House.

Dulary grew used to being with the grown-up elephants. Indeed, she must have felt that she was also grown-up. But she didn't forget Ann. Ann would come by many times to say hello and to pet Dulary's trunk just as she used to do.

Dulary was always glad to see Ann, but she didn't carry on and call after her when Ann went away. She was acting more grown-up.

Anyone could tell that she really wasn't a baby anymore.

Life away from the zoo might have been more thrilling, but not nearly so safe for Dulary. Here at the zoo she was safe and happy — and loved by all the children of Philadelphia.

(To be read by the teacher.)

The Secret Song

Who saw the petals
    drop from the rose?
I, said the spider,
But nobody knows.

Who saw the sunset
    flash on a bird?
I, said the fish,
But nobody heard.

Who saw the fog
    come over the sea?
I, said the sea pigeon,
Only me.

Who saw the first
    green light of the sun?
I, said the night owl,
The only one.

Who saw the moss
    creep over the stone?
I, said the grey fox,
All alone.

MARGARET WISE BROWN

132

WOULD YOU BELIEVE IT?

The world of nature is full of surprises. The more that you look at it and read about it, the more surprises you will find.

Did you know that there is a bird that can fly backwards? Did you know that bees can "talk" by dancing?

Here are a few of the many animals that make the world of nature such a strange and wonderful place.

133

Would you believe there's an animal that loves to slide down hills? It's the otter, one of the most fun-loving animals in the world.

Otters make their homes near rivers and lakes. There they have great fun in a most surprising way. Over and over again, summer and winter, they will slide down a hill on their stomachs!

If *you* like to slide or ski in the snow, you can guess how much fun the otters have in winter. They love a snowy hill. In the summer one of the things they like best is to slide downhill right into the water — splash!

An otter family at play — old and young together — is one of the great sights of the animal world.

Have you ever seen a pack rat's nest? It is a nest of twigs and leaves and junk. The pack rat will collect almost any little thing for its nest. It is always picking up small things and bringing them home to put with its junk collection. But the pack rat does something very strange. It always leaves something in trade for what it has taken. That is why it is called a trader rat as well as a pack rat.

Do you know what a bee does when it finds flowers? It flies home at once. Then it does a dance in front of the other bees. The dance tells the bees about the flowers and how to get to them.

The dance also lets the bees know how far away the flowers are. It even tells the other bees if there are a lot of flowers or only a few.

When the dance is over, many bees may fly away and go right to the flowers the first bee found!

Most people can walk backwards. But only one bird in the whole world can fly backwards—the hummingbird.

If you have ever watched hummingbirds feeding or seen them flying in a garden, you will know that they fly in a way very different from most birds.

This tiny, colorful bird can move straight up or straight down. It can even stay in the air in one spot without falling. And when the bird is feeding, it sometimes flies backwards for a second or two.

Would you believe there's a four-legged animal that does not walk, but can go faster on foot than most other animals? Would you believe that there is a bird with a bill longer than its body? Or a bug that looks just like a leaf? Well, there is. Look at the pictures below. Then you may want to do some reading on your own.

You may find many other surprises in the wonderful world of nature.

Biruté and the Orangutans

Meeting the Orangutans

Who is this woman? Her full name is Biruté Galdikas-Brindamour. She is living in the forests of Borneo.

Biruté and her husband, Rod Brindamour, came to Borneo from America. Why did they come to this wild, faraway place? Because Borneo is the home of the orangutans—and Biruté is a scientist who is studying them.

Biruté and Rod work together. Rod takes pictures. He took the ones you see here.

Orangutan means "person of the forest." Scientists call them "orangs" for short. Orangs are part of the Great Ape family, but they look and act like people in many ways. They learn things easily. They can walk on two legs; they have long arms, and their hands are like ours.

Of course, orangs are not people. And they are different from other Great Apes, too. Most Great Apes live together in groups, sharing and enjoying one another's company. Orangs do not do this. Only mother and baby orangutans live together. When the babies grow up, they move away and live by themselves in the forest.

Biruté has been studying the wild orangutans of Borneo since 1971. She started by walking in the forests, looking for orangs. When she saw one she would follow it for as long as she could. She made notes on how it acted and what it did. It was a hard way to study orangutans. But Biruté found out many new things this way.

It was once believed that wild orangs spend all their lives in trees and never come down to the ground. Biruté found that this is not so.

One day she was walking up a narrow path in the forest. Suddenly the path was blocked by a large orang walking along with its head down. Biruté stopped. The orang stopped. Biruté stared at the orang. And the orang stared at Biruté.

Biruté knew that orangs are very gentle and will not fight unless they have to. But what would this one do?

Suddenly the orang turned around, walked away, and disappeared into the tall grass. It seemed that the orang had been just as surprised as Biruté!

Biruté also discovered something else about orangs. Before going to sleep orangs make nests of leaves and branches in a tree. Scientists believed that orangs always made their sleeping nests high in trees. But Biruté discovered some orang nests on the ground. She found other nests on low logs not far from the ground.

People once believed that grown orangutans always live in the trees and never come down to the ground. This has been disproved by Biruté's studies of orangutans in Borneo.

Young Orangs in the Camp

Today orangutans are in danger of disappearing from the earth. The forests where orangs live are being cut down, leaving the orangs without homes. And people hunt for young orangs to sell as pets. In Borneo no one is allowed to keep pet orangs. But some people do. So now and then forest officers find orangs being kept as pets.

The officers want to return these orangs to the forest. But the young orangs do not know how to find food or build nests. They have never learned to care for themselves in the wild. They would die there. The officers sometimes send these orangs to Biruté's camp.

Biruté and Rod look after them. They train them to live in the wild forest. Biruté also studies them closely to learn how orangs act when they are young.

The first orangs in Biruté's camp were like very loving, *very* mischievous children. The youngest orangs loved Biruté. They held onto her and followed her everywhere. They shrieked if she went out of sight. They wanted to be with her every second of the day and night. Biruté had a hard time *ever* getting away from them. She couldn't even hide from the orangs in her hut. The hut was made out of weak bark, and the orangs got in easily.

One young orang who came to Biruté's camp was named Sugito. Sugito was very friendly and playful. He became great friends with the camp cat. Sugito liked to hold the big cat in his arms like a baby. He would kiss the cat; then he would place the cat on top of his head and smile a happy orangutan smile. Sometimes Sugito pulled the cat's legs—too hard. Out flew the cat's claws. Sugito squealed, and the cat raced off to a safe place.

The orangs seemed to have no end of tricks to play on Biruté and Rod. They would put salt in Biruté's tea when she was not looking. They would pick up pens and drink out all the ink. They pulled caps off pill bottles and gnawed on the pills. They even put some old socks into the teapot. And just for the fun of it, they sometimes filled their mouths with milk and sprayed it at each other.

Biruté knew that the orangs would never learn to live in the trees as long as they could sleep and eat and have fun in the camp hut.

After a time Rod built a stronger hut out of wood. The orangs could not get into this one.

The bark hut was left for the orangs, and they soon made a wreck of it. The orangs had no hut to live in. So they learned to build nests in the trees and find their own food. Soon they were able to live like other orangutans in the wild, wet forest. One by one the orangutans left Biruté's camp.

Biruté was happy that her orangs had learned to live in the forest. But sometimes she was sad that her shrieking, silly, playful, loving little orangs were gone.

148

Work at Biruté's camp in Borneo has not stopped. New orangs are sent there to be trained for life in the forest. And Biruté is still studying, making notes, and learning new things about them.

Work such as Biruté's has deepened our knowledge of this friendly, gentle ape. Her work may show what people must do to keep the orangutan from disappearing completely from the earth.

How Animals Rest

by MILLICENT SELSAM

While you lie in your bed at night, many of the animals outside are sleeping, too. Like you, they must rest. And each one has its own way of making itself comfortable.

150

Orangutans in the rainforest sleep high in treetops. They are at home in the trees and make their beds anywhere they happen to be when they're ready for sleep.

It's a shaky bed, and when the wind is blowing, the bed will rock. But the orangutans won't fall out. They know how to hang on even when the wind is fierce.

Some monkeys sleep in much the same way.

151

If you tried to sleep standing up, you'd fall down; but a giraffe can sleep standing up. It has a very, very long neck, which may hang down when the giraffe is sleeping. But sometimes, a sleeping giraffe rests its head against a tree.

When a very young giraffe rests, it has its own way of getting comfortable. It may lie down on the ground. Then it just turns its neck around and over and rests its neck on its back, so that its head is right over its back legs. It makes a very strange-looking giraffe that way.

Some elephants sleep standing up, but most elephants lie down. To get down they first go to their knees, then all the way down on their sides. You may have seen an elephant do this in a circus.

Any elephant that lies down to go to sleep has a lot of work to do when it wakes up. It has to get its big heavy body off the ground. It does this by rocking from side to side until it can roll up to its feet.

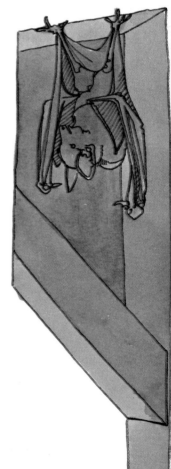

Many animals take their rest at night, just as you do. But some animals sleep in the daytime and wake up only when the sun sets.

The owl and the bat sleep by day and hunt by night. When a bat sleeps, it hangs upside down! The woodland owl sleeps sitting on a tree limb or inside the tree trunk.

Some animals sleep very little—they just doze off now and then. But in a very short time they wake up and are lively again.

Some fish cannot close their eyes, so it is hard to know if they ever really sleep. But we know when they are resting because sometimes they do not move at all.

You may hear now and then about the long winter sleep that some animals take. These animals *hibernate*. In this way they can last out even a severe winter, one with great cold and heavy snows. While deer and foxes are hunting in the snow for food, these animals just sleep the winter away.

The frogs that you see near a pond in summer hibernate in winter. They lie in a deep sleep at the bottom of the pond. Night and day they do not move; their hearts work very, very slowly. The frogs do not need to eat when they are hibernating.

Other animals hibernate, too, but their sleep is lighter.

In the autumn chipmunks eat a lot to store up food in their bodies. And they store away more food where they are going to sleep.

During the long winter these hibernating chipmunks will wake up every now and then to eat a little something. On a sunny day they may even run around outside for a bit. Then they return to their comfortable winter home, lie down, turn over, and go back to sleep.

Find the Main Idea

Which monkey is telling the most important thing about the picture? If you said the monkey on the right, you are correct. It is telling the *main idea* of the picture.

Many paragraphs have main ideas, too. The main idea of a paragraph is the most important thing it tells. It is what most of the sentences are about.

Read the paragraph on the next page. See if you can find the main idea.

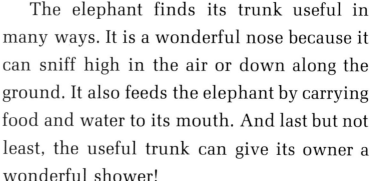

The elephant finds its trunk useful in many ways. It is a wonderful nose because it can sniff high in the air or down along the ground. It also feeds the elephant by carrying food and water to its mouth. And last but not least, the useful trunk can give its owner a wonderful shower!

What is the main idea? Did you see that it is stated in the first sentence? The main idea is often stated in the first sentence of a paragraph. But sometimes it is stated in another sentence.

Read the following paragraph and find the sentence that states the main idea.

Most mammals have noses and lips, but the platypus has a bill like a duck. It has no teeth at all. And long webs of skin grow between its toes. The platypus is a most unusual-looking mammal.

Which sentence states the main idea? In this paragraph, it's the last sentence.

Finding Details

Reread the paragraph about the elephant's trunk on page 158. You know that the first sentence is important because it states the main idea. But the other sentences are important, too. They give *details* about the main idea. Each detail tells something about the main idea.

What details are given in the paragraph that tell about the elephant's trunk?

Now read the paragraph on the next page. The main idea is stated in the first sentence. Look carefully at the other sentences. Can you find a detail that does *not* explain the main idea?

Leaping is the kangaroo's way of getting from one place to another. At usual speed, the leaps of a large kangaroo are about one and a half meters long. Most kangaroos are found in Australia. When a kangaroo runs from danger, its leaps may be as long as seven and a half meters!

Which sentence does not explain the main idea? If you leave this sentence out, does the paragraph make better sense?

 **TRY THIS**

1. Find the sentence that states the main idea in the paragraph below.
2. Find the detail that does *not* explain the main idea.
3. How do the rest of the details explain the main idea?

Every kind of animal has special ways to defend itself. Some animals hide when they are in danger. Some play dead. Many run from their enemies. Some animals are easily tamed. Others have built-in armor to protect them.

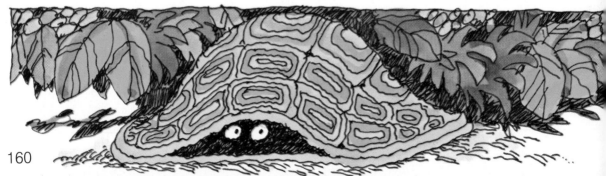

Just for Fun

The Man Who Didn't Wash His Dishes

by PHYLLIS KRASILOVSKY

There once was a man who lived by himself. He cooked his own food, he made his own bed, and he cleaned the house and kept it clean, all by himself.

One night the man came home from the station—the bus station where he worked—and he was very hungry. He was so hungry he fixed a bigger supper than he had ever fixed before. It was very good supper, too.

But the man was tired, very tired by the time he'd finished eating. He was ready to rest.

He really didn't want to do the dishes. He wished he had a machine to wash them, as some people had. The dishes had to be done by hand, and he felt he was much too tired to go over and do them.

Well, the man leaned back in the chair, as full as could be, and thought. He said to himself that he'd leave the dishes this one time. Just this one time. He'd leave them till the next night, and then he would wash them all at once.

But the next night he was very hungry, so he cooked a lot. He used a lot of dishes for supper, and he was *very tired* when he was done. He just couldn't *face* all those dirty dishes! He had worked hard at the station all day, and that pile of dirty dishes was just too much for a tired person to do. So he left all the dishes in the sink once again.

As the days went by, the dirty dishes piled up. They kept on piling up, too. The man was always very hungry every night, and then always very tired after supper. So he never could face the dishes.

After a time there were so many dirty dishes that the sink was full. The man began to pile them here and there around the house.

They kept on piling up and piling up, and leaning on each other, everywhere. Soon the floor was so full that the man had a hard time getting around in the house.

At last the man discovered that there wasn't one clean dish left in the house. Not one. Did he wash the dishes, then? No! He ate out of

pots and pans till they were all dirty, too. After *that* he used some clean new flowerpots that he happened to have.

Finally he used up *everything*. And he didn't know what to do. What's more, he couldn't *find* anything anymore. He couldn't find the books that he wanted to read. He couldn't see the pictures on the wall. He couldn't find a chair to sit in. And he couldn't even find his bed.

Then the lights went out, and he could not find the light fixtures to put some new lights in them. It was *horrible*. Everything was hidden by a *mountain* of dishes. And he couldn't find the sink so he could wash them!

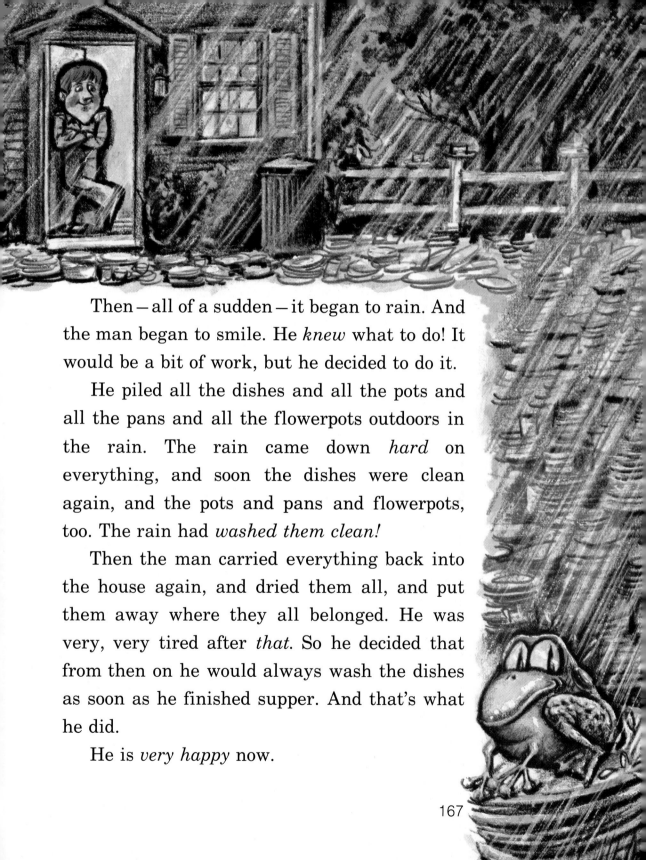

Then—all of a sudden—it began to rain. And the man began to smile. He *knew* what to do! It would be a bit of work, but he decided to do it.

He piled all the dishes and all the pots and all the pans and all the flowerpots outdoors in the rain. The rain came down *hard* on everything, and soon the dishes were clean again, and the pots and pans and flowerpots, too. The rain had *washed them clean!*

Then the man carried everything back into the house again, and dried them all, and put them away where they all belonged. He was very, very tired after *that.* So he decided that from then on he would always wash the dishes as soon as he finished supper. And that's what he did.

He is *very happy* now.

Little Hatchy Hen

by JAMES FLORA

"Tell me a story, Grandfather," said Carla.

"All right," said Grandfather, "I'll tell one about a hen your grandmother once had. We've had many hens in our time. But this was a really wonderful hen. We called her Little Hatchy Hen."

This is the story that Grandfather told.

Grandma's little hen laid lots of eggs. Then she would hatch them. There was nothing Little Hatchy Hen liked better than sitting on eggs and hatching them out. She was a very good hatcher—no matter what kinds of eggs you put in her nest, she would hatch them. She could hatch ducks, and bluebirds, and once she even hatched a turtle.

One time Grandma put some flour in the nest. Believe it or not, that Little Hatchy Hen hatched some bread. That's how we found out that Hatchy Hen could hatch out almost anything we put in her nest.

First we put a doorknob under her. And what do you know, she hatched out a new front door. It had a window and curtains and a nice coat of red paint.

We put an old clock in Hatchy Hen's nest, and she hatched out twenty wrist watches. Grandma and I gave them away as birthday presents.

Whenever Grandma needed a new dress, she would put a tiny piece of cloth in the nest. First thing you knew, the little red hen would hatch out the prettiest dress you ever did see.

There didn't seem to be anything that little hen couldn't hatch. If you put a tire and a steering wheel under her, she would hatch out a fine new car.

Once Hatchy Hen found some wood and some nails. She put them in her nest and hatched out a whole new henhouse for herself. She was a very handy hen to have around the farm.

Of course, we could never be sure just what Hatchy Hen would hatch out of things. Once when Grandma was going on a trip, she needed a new trunk for her clothes. So she put a little box under Hatchy Hen and said, "Now hatch me a nice new trunk."

Hatchy Hen hatched her a trunk all right. But it wasn't the kind of trunk Grandma wanted. It was an elephant's trunk, with a whole elephant

hooked up with it. Grandma used it anyway — she said it was better than a clothes trunk.

Another time I remember, I had baskets and baskets of fruit to take to market. But I had no way to carry them there. I thought how nice it would be to have a train of my own, so I put a bell and a whistle in Hatchy Hen's nest. I waited and waited, and she hatched and hatched.

The nest got bigger and bigger, and I was sure she was hatching a train. But she didn't. Do you know what she hatched? She hatched a boat — and we lived a hundred miles from the nearest river. I never did get to use that boat.

The best thing Hatchy Hen ever did was the time she saved the whole farm. One dark Tuesday night in July, Grandma and I woke up, and we could hear Hatchy Hen shouting: KUT-KUT-KA-DAW-KUT!

We looked out the window. The barn was on fire. I ran out and turned on the hose to put out the fire, but the hose was too short. The water wouldn't reach the fire. The barn would surely burn.

Grandma ran into the house and got Hatchy Hen. She filled her nest with spaghetti and put the hen on top. "Now, hatch, little hen," she said, "hatch in a hurry."

Hatchy Hen sat down in the nest and started to hatch. In a little while she was through and hopped off the nest. And what do you think she had hatched out of that spaghetti?

Fire hose. A hundred meters of fire hose. I hooked it up to the water and put out the fire. That's how Hatchy Hen saved the farm.

Some Funny Poems

Way down South where the coconuts grow,
A little ant stepped on an elephant's toe.
The elephant cried, with tears in his eyes,
"Pick on somebody your own size."

I always eat peas with honey,
I've done it all my life.
They do taste kind of funny
But it keeps them on the knife.

175

There was a Young Man on a plain
Who wandered about in the rain.
   He said: "Well, what OF it?
   I LOVE it! I LOVE it!"
And he said so again and again.

WILLIAM JAY SMITH

176

The Panther

The panther is like a leopard,
Except it hasn't been peppered.
Should you behold a panther crouch,
Prepare to say Ouch.
Better yet, if called by a panther,
Don't anther.

OGDEN NASH

177

Two Limericks

A Tutor

A tutor who tootled the flute
    Was teaching two tooters to toot.
Said the two to the tutor,
    "Is it harder to toot,
Or to tutor two tooters to toot?"

CAROLYN WELLS

A pleasant old bear at the zoo
Said, "I always find something to do.
When it bores me, you know,
To walk to and fro,
I change it and walk fro and to."

178

The Lazy People

Let's write a poem about lazy people
Who lazily laze their lives away;
Let's finish it tomorrow,
I'm much too tired today.

SHEL SILVERSTEIN

Miss Louisa and the Outlaws

by FRANCES B. WATTS

The People

Sheriff

Benny the Bad

Dirty Dan

Betty Ann

Harris

Maria

Miss Louisa

Jane

Other Children

The Time

About a hundred years ago.

The Place

A schoolhouse in the Old West. The youngest children sit in the front, and the older ones sit at the back of the room. Miss Louisa, the teacher, is standing in front of the room.

MISS LOUISA: All right, is everyone ready to listen?

CHILDREN (*loudly*): Yes, Miss Louisa.

MISS LOUISA (*smiling*): Now, then, I'll read a story to you.

(*Miss Louisa opens her book and starts to read out loud. Just then, two big men with guns come through the door. The children get out of their seats and run to Miss Louisa.*)

MEN: Stay where you are, all of you!

(*The children's eyes open wide with fear; Miss Louisa, though, is fearless. She looks straight at the two men. A girl named Jane leans over to talk to her friend Harris.*)

JANE: They're *outlaws!* It's Benny the Bad and Dirty Dan! They robbed the River City Bank last summer!

HARRIS: You're right. I saw their pictures all around town. Wanted, the signs said. They're wanted men!

MISS LOUISA: Goodness, children, please go back to your seats and sit down.

DIRTY DAN: The boy's right. Everyone set down—nobody's going to get hurt, as long as all of you set there quiet.

MISS LOUISA: Children, I believe this person means you must *sit there quietly.*

DAN: Hmmm? Well, just *sit there quietly.*

MISS LOUISA: Now, what do you want here in our schoolhouse?

BENNY THE BAD: Well, Miss, Dan and me, we're going to hide out right here till the freight train comes through. Then we'll make our getaway. It won't be long now, so don't anybody do anything bright like shouting out the window or trying to be helpful to the Sheriff!

(Benny waves the gun around.)

MISS LOUISA: Stop waving that gun at helpless people. If you're not more careful, it may go off and hurt one of the children. And do sit down at once.

BENNY: Say, what's this? We don't have to do what you say.

MISS LOUISA: As long as you are in this schoolhouse, you do; I am the teacher here. Sit down, the two of you!

(*Slowly, the outlaws sit.*)

MISS LOUISA: Very good. And remember, you must be quiet while you are here.

DAN: Listen here, you—!

MISS LOUISA: I said *quiet!* Do you want to stay here or not?

(*The two outlaws look at each other.*)

DAN: Oh, all right, all right.

MISS LOUISA: Thank you. Hmmm, it's getting darkish out—it looks as if it might rain. We must take our flag down. Jane, will you and Betty Ann go out and bring in the flag?

BENNY: No, you don't! They'll run to the Sheriff. You can't fool us. Nobody's ever made us look foolish, so don't count on doing it now!

MISS LOUISA: Sir, we do *not* fly our flag when it looks like rain.

(At this, some of the children look at each other in surprise.)

JANE: Miss Louisa, I don't want to go outside. It really doesn't look like rain.

MISS LOUISA: Jane, there are some large clouds coming this way. *(To outlaws)* One of you may go with the children if you wish. You can help them take down the flag.

(Benny goes out with Betty Ann and Jane.)

MISS LOUISA: Let's have a spelling bee, girls and boys. Harris and Maria may start picking two teams.

(Harris and Maria call out children's names, and the teams line up on different sides of the room.)

MARIA: I pick Dan.

185

(*Dan looks pleased; he gets in line and puts the gun away. Miss Louisa calls out words, and the boys and girls and Dan take turns. Benny, Jane, and Betty Ann come in with the flag, and Betty Ann puts it away.*)

BENNY: Say, what's going on here?

DAN: It's a spelling bee—haven't you ever been in a spelling bee?

BENNY: No, and I'm not going to start that foolishness now. We've got to watch for the freight train.

MISS LOUISA: I understand; it would be terrible if the children all spelled better than you did, wouldn't it?

BENNY: Who's scared of spelling some old words? I haven't been to school much, but I can spell fine.

DAN: Then get in line over there. It's fun.

(*Benny joins Harris's team.*)

MISS LOUISA: Benny, spell "robber."

BENNY (*surprised*): Uh—uh—let's see. Uh, R–O. R–O–O–B–E–R.

MISS LOUISA: Sorry, Benny—"robber" is spelled with two *b*'s, not two *o*'s.

(Benny's face wears a foolish look; he kicks his foot against the wall and hangs his head. The sound of a train is heard; Dan runs to the window.)

DAN: Oh no, there goes the freight train! What should we do?

(The outlaws look very angry.)

BENNY: I knew we had to keep watch. Why did you get me into that silly game?

MARIA: You're just angry because you missed your word.

(Benny turns around fast and waves a gun as Miss Louisa moves to stand in front of her children.)

MISS LOUISA: Please have the politeness not to wave that gun in front of my children!

BENNY: Sorry, Miss Louisa.

(*Suddenly the Sheriff runs into the room, catching the outlaws by surprise.*)

SHERIFF: Hands up!

(*The outlaws put their hands high.*)

BETTY ANN (*calls out*): Sheriff, how did you know the outlaws were here?

SHERIFF: I didn't know, but I thought that something was wrong when I saw that the school flag wasn't flying. Why, Miss Louisa never lowers that flag till the sun goes down unless it's raining real hard. She never takes it down for a few clouds. I've always known that—she was my teacher, too, you know. Let's go, you two.

BENNY (*as he goes out*): That teacher, she sure don't scare easy!

MISS LOUISA: You're right, Benny. A person like you who tries to scare young children could never scare me.

(*Benny looks hurt. The Sheriff leads the outlaws away. The children crowd around Miss Louisa; she sits down and holds her head in her hands.*)

JANE: Miss Louisa, were you afraid when the outlaws were here?

MISS LOUISA: Oh, yes, very much afraid.

BETTY ANN: You didn't act scared.

MISS LOUISA: Sometimes we have to act fearlessly, even when we're afraid.

BETTY ANN: Miss Louisa, we're proud of you!

HARRIS: I'll say we are!

ALL: Hurray for Miss Louisa!

189

Double Meanings

What should the woman do? Can you tell?

Words often mean more than one thing. The word *right* means "That is true." It also means "the opposite of *left*." Here are some more words that mean more than one thing.

Did you know that:

1. Someone who says "Come *back*" is not talking to a part of the body?

2. Someone can *beat* you without touching you?

3. To *join a club*, you do not have to put two pieces of a broken stick together?

4. If someone yells *"Duck!"* you should take cover instead of looking for a bird?

Can you tell the two meanings of *back*, *beat*, *club*, and *duck*?

Many words have more than one meaning. Sometimes you can tell what a word means by the way it is used in the sentence. Read this sentence:

Be careful not to trip on your mountain-climbing trip.

You know that *trip* can mean to "stumble" or "fall." It can also mean "a journey." By the way the words are used in the sentence, you can figure out what each *trip* means.

Now look at this picture. What does the word *kind* mean in each sentence?

If you look up the word *kind* in the dictionary or glossary, you would find out that it has more than one meaning. It means "sort" or "type"; it also means "willing to help" or "friendly."

People like to make jokes with words that have two meanings. These jokes are called *puns.* Have you heard this pun?

Why did the baker grow angry at the bread? Because it was so fresh!

Do you see how this joke uses two meanings of *fresh?* Look up the word *fresh* in your dictionary to find the two meanings.

Find the word in each pun that has a double meaning. Use a dictionary to find what each meaning is.

1. Why did the teacher wear dark glasses?
   Because she had a very bright class.
2. Did anyone laugh when you fell on the ice?
   No, but the ice made a few cracks.
3. Why did Humpty Dumpty have a great fall?
   Because he had such an awful summer.

Wonders of the World

(To be read by the teacher.)

Swift things are beautiful:
Swallows and deer,
And lightning that falls
Bright-veined and clear,
Rivers and meteors,
Wind in the wheat,
The strong-withered horse,
The runner's sure feet.

And slow things are beautiful:
The closing of day,
The pause of the wave
That curves downward to spray,
The ember that crumbles,
The opening flower,
And the ox that moves on
In the quiet of power.

ELIZABETH COATSWORTH

Hole in the Ground!

This rocky canyon, a kilometer and a half deep, is the deepest and widest cut ever discovered on the earth. We call it the Grand Canyon. The name is a good one. The canyon is truly grand in every way.

196

You can stand on the rim of the canyon and look out and down at the canyon walls. You can see walls of brightly colored rock and walls with grasses and trees growing on them.

You see that the walls have many layers of different-colored rocks. You can see pinks and reds and yellows. You see brown and shiny gold and white— many, many colors! As the sun rises and sets, the colors of the canyon walls change as if by magic.

They change all the time in the changing light of day. The deepest colors are seen at sundown. Then shadows fill the canyon, and stars begin to come out in the deep blue sky.

A Cut in the Earth

What made this big cut in the earth? What kind of tool could cut into layers of hard rock?

You can see it there, on the bottom of the canyon. It is now a kilometer and a half below the canyon rims. It is a river, running down to the sea.

Millions of years ago this river ran slowly across a plain. Then little by little some of the land began to rise, making a high place in the path of the river. The land came up so slowly that the river cut right through it.

The land kept rising, and the river kept on cutting through it. So the canyon walls got higher and higher.

As the river ran down to the sea, it moved faster and faster. It picked up sand and rocks and carried them along. The rushing river and all it carried began to dig into the earth, and so the river bed grew wider and deeper.

Rains fell, making new streams. The streams fell over the steep walls into the river, so the river got bigger. And on and on it ran.

It took the river a long, long time to make the canyon we know today. It took more than ten million years.

Today many people go down the river in boats. They go through the whirlpools and the madly rushing water just for fun.

Other people like to walk down into the canyon along the rocky path. People ride down, too. It is a long, hard, steep trip to the canyon floor. It takes all day to go down and back.

The Earth's Past in the Canyon Walls

The Grand Canyon is important to scientists who study the earth. They learn many things from the rock layers. The scientists study the rock layers from bottom to top. In this way they can find out what the earth has been like in the past. They can read the earth's early "story" in the rock.

The first, or bottom, layer is the oldest. Scientists think it is about two billion years old—that is, two thousand million years.

Other rock layers formed on top of the first one. Still others formed on top of those. The top layers are the newest—they were formed last of all.

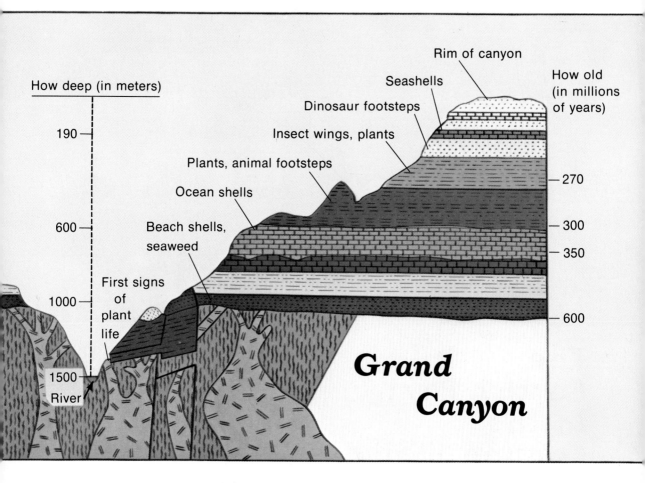

Each rock layer was laid down by wind and by seas of times long past. In some layers there are shells, animal teeth, or fossils. Fossils are plants or animals of the past hardened in earth or rock. Different rock layers in the canyon have different fossils.

Some layers have fossils of animals that once lived in long-ago seas. Other layers have fossils of dinosaurs and other land animals that died out millions of years ago.

Some layers have no fossils at all. Maybe there were no living things when those layers were formed. Or maybe the living things of that time were so soft, there was nothing left of them after the rock formed.

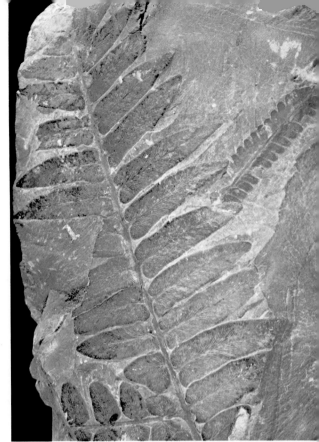

Many fossils like these have been found in the rock layers of the Grand Canyon.

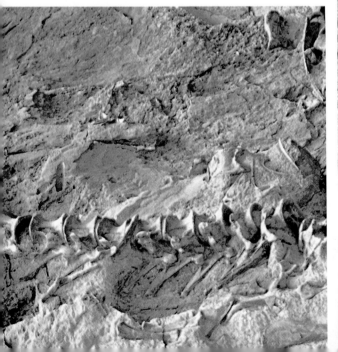

It took the river millions of years to make the Grand Canyon. Today the Grand Canyon is so grand, so important, and so beautiful that it has been made into a national park. The Grand Canyon belongs to all the people of America, and it has been called the one great sight everyone in America should see.

Canyon Models to Make

You can make a good model of the Grand Canyon if you have a little outdoor space to use. You will need a hose or a large watering can; you will also need boxes of different kinds of sand, soil, and some clay or mud.

If you like, you can color white sand with water-color paint. Look at a picture of the Grand Canyon and make the sand the colors of the rock. You'll want a number of different colors.

Build a hill by putting down layers of different colors. Pack them tightly together. Mud or clay layers will help to hold the other layers together.

You may want to put make-believe fossils in some layers. If so, stick shells or pieces of shells in one layer. Put bits of bark, leaves, and seeds in another layer; put small feathers in another. Different kinds of grasses can go in another layer. You will easily think of other things to use as make-believe fossils.

Lay a few rocks on top of your hill. Then let water from the watering can or from the hose be a river. Can your river cut a canyon through the hill? Be sure that the colors of the layers show in your canyon's walls.

You may have to build your canyon more than once before you get it just right.

How deep and wide can you make your canyon?

You can make a different kind of canyon model indoors. Study the pictures carefully before you start.

You'll need a pack of colored paper. Use a good, strong, stiff paper, the heavyweight kind. Sort out the colors before you start your model: put all the reds together, all the yellows together, and so on.

Start the model with a piece of blue paper. This will be the river at the bottom of your canyon.

Now you are ready for your rock layers. Pick any color for the bottom layer — maybe a dark red would be good to start with. This layer, remember, is put down first.

Tear a small pile of the dark red paper the long way. Make your pieces look like those in the picture.

Put the two parts of your first layer down on the blue paper. Be sure to leave some space between the two parts so that your river shows.

Next tear another color to put on top of your first layer.

Keep adding layers of color, in the way shown in the picture. Remember to use a different color each time. You'll soon have a small model of a canyon with many-colored walls.

Add some little rocks on the top to hold the paper down, and then show how things grow above the canyon. You can use some small models of trees and other plants, or you can make cutout trees, or you can use tiny twigs and grasses. Think of other things you can do to show what the canyon looks like.

THE HILL OF FIRE

by THOMAS P. LEWIS

Once there was a farmer who lived in
Mexico. He lived in a little village, in a house
which had only one room. The farmer was not
happy. "Nothing ever happens," he said.

The people in the village thought the farmer
was foolish. "We have everything we need,"
they said. "We have a school, and a market, and
a church with an old bell that rings on Sundays.
Our village is the best there is."

"But nothing ever happens," said the
farmer.

Every morning, when the farmer woke up,
the first thing he saw was the roof of his little

211

house. Every morning he ate two flat cakes of ground corn along with some tea. "Nothing ever happens," he said.

It was still dark and the farmer got ready to leave for the field. His son Pablo was still sleeping.

"Maybe today," said his wife, "something will happen."

"No," said the farmer, "nothing will." The farmer walked away with his ox and did not look back.

At night the farmer returned. He gave some food to his ox, and then he sat down by the fire. Pablo played with five smooth stones, throwing them at a hole he had dug in the earth. "See, Father," said Pablo, "I got one in!" But the farmer was tired. He did not answer. Every day was the same.

One morning the farmer woke up very early, pulled on his shirt, and took his big hat from a peg on the wall. "I must go to the field early," he said. "The plowing is not done, and soon it will be time to plant the corn."

All morning the farmer worked in his field. The ox helped him. When there was a big rock in the way, the ox stopped and lay down. The farmer pushed the rock away.

"Up! Up!" said the farmer. Then the ox got up and pulled again.

Late in the morning, when the sun was high, Pablo came to the field.

"Pablo!" said the farmer. "Why are you not in school?"

"There is no school today, Father," said Pablo. "I have come to help you plow."

The farmer smiled. He reached into his pocket and gave the boy a small toy made of wood.

"Thank you!" cried Pablo. The farmer had made it for his son during the hot time of the day when he rested from his work.

Pablo helped the farmer plow the field. The ox pulled, and the plow turned up the soil. Suddenly the plow stopped. The farmer and his son pushed, and the ox pulled, but the plow did not move. It fell into the earth. It went down, down, down, into a little hole. There was a noise deep under the ground, as if something big had growled.

The farmer looked. Pablo looked. The ox turned its head. White smoke came from the hole in the ground.

"Run!" said the farmer. "Run!"

There was a loud CRACK and the earth opened wide. The farmer ran, Pablo ran, and the ox ran too. Fire and smoke came from the ground. The farmer ran all the way to the village. He ran into the church and rang the old bell.

The other farmers came from their fields. People came out of their houses. "Look!" said the farmer. "Look there!"

That night no one could sleep. Everyone watched the fire in the sky. It came from where the farmer's field had been. There was a loud BOOM, and another, and another.

Hot lava came out of the earth. The lava twisted over the ground, through the trees. It came toward the farmer's house. It came toward the village. Pieces of burning stone flew in the air. The earth coughed. Every time it coughed, the hill of fire grew bigger.

In a few days the hill was as big as a mountain. And every now and then there was a loud BOOM. Squirrels and rabbits ran, and birds flew away from the fire. People took their animals away to safe places. Burning pieces of rock flew everywhere. The farmer and his neighbors put wet cloths over their noses to keep out the smoke.

When the booming stopped and the fires dwindled, the farmer's house was gone. The school was gone. The market was gone. Half the village was gone.

One day some soldiers came in cars and trucks. "So you are the one with the plow that opened up the earth," they said to the farmer. They laughed. "You are lucky to be living, my friend." The soldiers looked at the village. An officer spoke. "Everyone must go! It is not safe to live here any longer."

The farmer and his wife and Pablo and all the people of the village went away in trucks. They went with the soldiers.

The farmer found a new house. It was bigger

than the one they lived in before. It was not far from the old one, but it was far enough away to be safe from *El Monstruo*. That is the name the people gave to the great volcano.

The people made a new village. They made a new school and a new market. Then they had a great party, because they were safe. At the party the band played, and the people danced and danced.

Now the farmer had a new field. Every morning he woke up early. It was still dark, and the volcano was glowing in the sky. Every morning he ate two flat cakes of ground corn along with his tea. Then the farmer went to his new field. His ox went with him, just as before.

Sometimes Pablo brought the children of the village to see the farmer. From the field they could see the volcano smoking.

"Can you make another hill of fire?" the children said.

"No, my friends, no, no," said the farmer. He laughed. "One hill of fire is enough for me."

Visitors from Space

On a summer night you may see what looks like a falling star. But that is not a star, for stars do not fall or shoot across the sky. Stars are like our sun—they are much too large and too far away to move swiftly across the sky.

What look like falling or shooting stars are meteors from outer space. Most of them are tiny rocks which shoot around in space, too many of them to be counted.

As long as meteors stay in space, you cannot see them. But once they hit the earth's atmosphere, they start to heat up. As these meteors rub against the air, they get hotter and hotter, glow brightly, and move fast. When they are glowing white-hot, we can see them, and we call them "shooting stars."

After a very short time, a meteor's light dies out. This happens because the meteor has burned up. Most of the time meteors burn in the air, long before they get down to the earth.

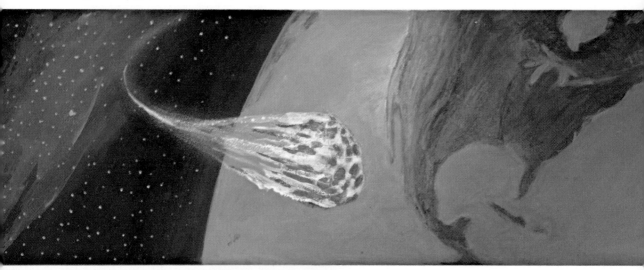

Once in a great while, a large meteor hits the earth's atmosphere and does not burn up completely on the way down. It hits the earth, and hits it hard. Then it is no longer called a meteor—it is called a meteorite.

When a big meteorite hits the ground, it makes a deep hole and keeps on going down. It may go so far under the ground that it is never found. We then have only the hole, or crater, to show that something from outer space has landed.

The crater you see in the picture is in Arizona. It was made by a meteorite that landed here in prehistoric times, many thousands of years ago. The hole is about one kilometer and a half across and about two hundred meters deep.

The Arizona crater is one of the two biggest meteorite craters on the earth; the largest one is in Canada. Those two craters are so big you

been found and taken from the earth. Meteorites and pieces of meteorites have been collected from many different parts of the world.

might look right at them with disbelief. The meteorites that made these giant craters must have been very big!

Not all meteorites are hidden underground. Many have

One of the best collections is in a museum in New York City. The picture above shows one of the large meteorites in that museum's meteorite collection.

Meteorites have been under study for many, many years. They have been looked at, cut open, and studied in all kinds of ways. We know now that some are made of rock, some of metal, and some of rock and metal together. Our knowledge in this field of study is still incomplete. There is much more that scientists want to find out.

Until a short time ago, meteorites were the only things from outer space that we could study, for they were all we had. Now we have moon rocks, carried back to the earth by people who landed on the moon.

Thanks to those moon trips, we also have pictures that give us a good look at some of the craters that are on the moon.

The picture shows part of one side of the moon. This is the side that we on the ground never see; it's always turned away from the earth. Take a good look—do you think that meteorites hit the moon as well as the earth?

Yes, they do. Scientists believe that many of the moon's craters were made in this way.

As more and more people go to the moon, we hope to learn more and more about the craters.

Do more meteorites hit the moon than hit the earth? From pictures of the moon, you really might think so; but the pictures are misleading. Scientists have learned that the earth has had many, many meteorite craters. They are unsure of the number, for most of the craters can no longer be seen. Craters on the earth do not last very long. They wear down because they are blown by the

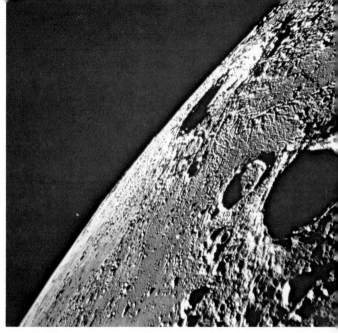

wind and washed away by the rain and snow; in time, grasses, trees, and other plants grow over them.

How different things are on the moon! There is no air, so no wind can blow; there is no water to fall as rain or snow. And of course, without air and rain, plants do not grow. There is very little to wear down or to hide the craters on the moon. Then, too, the meteors that fall to the moon cannot burn up in any air on the way down.

Every day millions of meteors come rushing into the earth's atmosphere. They make beautiful patterns of light in the sky, and then they die. They are visitors from outer space, but hardly ever do they touch the earth.

(To be read by the teacher.)

NIGHT

Stars over snow
  And in the west a planet
Swinging below a star —
  Look for a lovely thing and you will find it,
It is not far —
  It never will be far.

SARA TEASDALE

Comets

by JENE LYON

About two or three times in your life, you may be able to see a comet. A comet is a beautiful sight as it crosses the sky like a rocket. It leaves behind a trail of light that may be millions of kilometers long.

Comets follow long, loop-like paths. They come near the sun at one end and go far out past the rim of the Solar System at the other end.

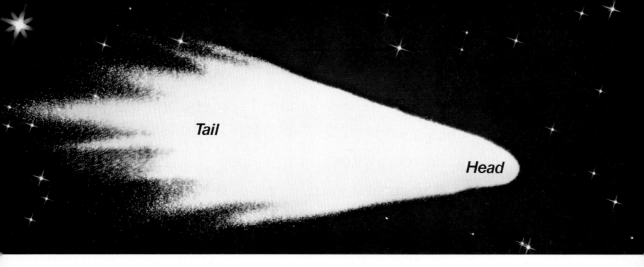

Tail

Head

The main part of a comet is the head. This is a ball of loosely held stony material, dust, and gas. It is much smaller than the earth.

When a comet comes near the sun, the sun's rays hit the head, push some gases out of it, and make them glow colorfully. This long train of gases is the tail of the comet. Some comets have two tails; a few have more. One comet had nine!

The tail of a comet always points away from the sun. The pressure of the sun's rays pushes it away. As the comet moves far away from the sun, the tail disappears.

There are thousands of comets, but only a few are big enough or come near enough to the earth to be seen without a telescope.

When first seen, a comet is a light spot in the dark sky. Night by night it grows brighter as it comes nearer and nearer to the sun. After weeks

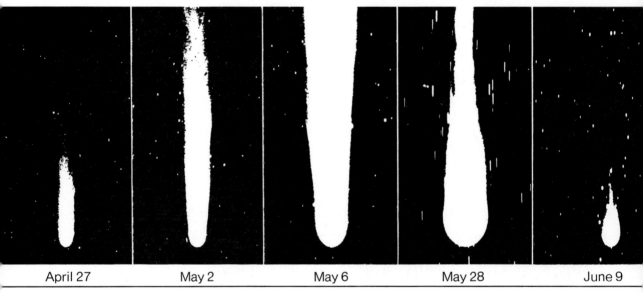

| April 27 | May 2 | May 6 | May 28 | June 9 |

or months it is at its brightest. Then it slowly dies as it moves away from the sun into outer space.

Some comets return again and again. But many keep moving in space without nearing the earth again. A few comets do break up, and some of these fall to the earth as meteors.

The best known comet is Halley's Comet. The path it moves along was worked out by Edmund

Halley in 1682. About every 77 years this comet returns to our part of the Solar System. It was last seen in the year 1910.

The gases in a comet's tail are very light. The stars can easily be seen through the tail. Once when the tail of Halley's Comet passed over the earth, no one but the scientists even knew it. But if the comet head had hit us, it would have been a different story!

A long time ago people thought comets brought bad luck. So they carefully recorded comet visits. Such records tell us that Halley's Comet was seen almost 2,000 years ago. If you wait, you may have a chance to see it the next time it passes our way.

Maria Mitchell

"An eclipse of the sun," Maria said to herself. It was daytime, but the sky grew darker and darker. The quiet seemed to grow, too, touching all the animals on the island. Maria counted the seconds and noted the stillness. Birds, cows, horses, and dogs stood quietly, wondering at the strange darkness that was covering them. And still the sky grew blacker and blacker. And still Maria counted the seconds and watched through a piece of smoked glass as the moon covered more and more of the sunlight.

Now the sun was covered, with only the bright rim showing. Maria stopped counting and wrote down the time in her notebook. She looked around at the heavy darkness that was covering the earth.

"No wonder people have always been scared by eclipses," she thought. And in the deep stillness, Maria seemed to hear the sound of her own heart.

It was a winter day in 1831, and young Maria Mitchell was with her father in their house on Nantucket Island. Her father had set up a telescope at the window and was looking through it as the moon moved away from the sun. The light returned.

Maria again wrote the time in her notebook. As she did, she was surprised by all the joyous noises she was hearing. All around her animals were barking, crowing, and singing. They were happy to have back the light.

Maria thought about how strange she'd felt watching the eclipse. The sun, the stars, and the moon had seemed so powerful to her. Why, people could not live without them!

Maria decided then that she would learn all she could about the skies. She did not know it at the time, but one day, her knowledge of the skies would make her one of the most famous astronomers in the world.

Many people in Nantucket were interested in the sun and the stars and the moon. Nantucket is right on the ocean, and many people who lived there were sailors. The position of the stars in the sky helped sailors find their way on the ocean. Maria's father was not a sailor, but stars were his great interest. He was well-known on the island for his great knowledge of the night skies.

In the years that followed the eclipse, Maria spent almost as much time on top of her house as in it. Each day after she finished her school work, she did her part of the housework. Then she followed her father to the roof, where he kept the telescope. They took turns looking at the stars through it. Sometimes in winter Maria's fingers and toes got very cold. The strong wind cut through her heavy coat and shook the telescope.

But Maria found the time enjoyable. She didn't let the cold or the wind stop her from learning about the stars.

Maria left school when she was sixteen and went to work as a teacher. Later she became a librarian. She was happy working in the library, for she loved books as much as she loved the skies. At the library Maria found time to study on her own and to teach herself what she needed to know to become an astronomer. For many years Maria's life had three parts: housework, library work, and sky work.

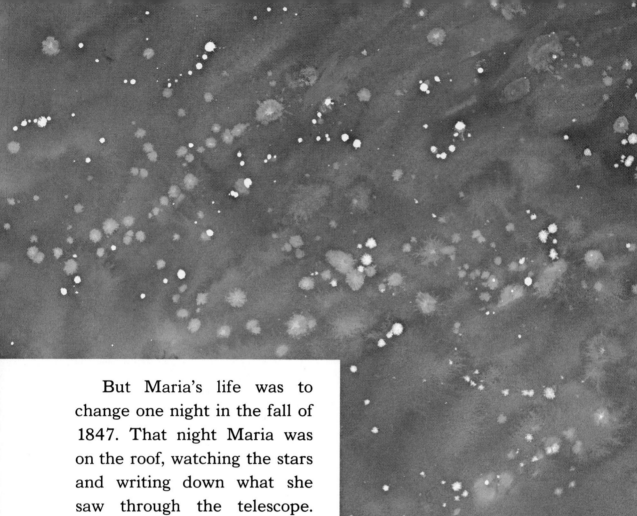

But Maria's life was to change one night in the fall of 1847. That night Maria was on the roof, watching the stars and writing down what she saw through the telescope. Suddenly she saw a small white spot in the sky. Was it a star? No, it couldn't be that. Maria knew the positions of the stars as well as she knew her own room.

What could it be? Maria closed her eyes. Then she opened them and looked again. It was still there: a tiny white spot! Though it was tiny, it was important because she had never seen it in the skies before. Quickly she wrote down the time, 10:30, and the position of the white spot in the sky.

Maria ran to her father, who was at a party downstairs. She talked softly for a few seconds. He looked surprised, left with her, and they ran up to the roof together.

He looked through the telescope at the white spot. Then he looked at a book showing the positions of the stars. At last he said to Maria, "Yes, you *have* discovered a comet!"

A comet! Comets are very hard to spot, even today. In that day, discovering a comet —spotting it before anyone else in the world did—was the hope of many astronomers. The telescopes of that time were not as strong as those we have today. The person who discovered a comet while it was still far from the earth had to be a remarkable astronomer, as Maria was.

News of Maria's discovery went around the world. Letters from astronomers came back to her. They said that no one else in the whole world spotted the comet until two nights after Maria did.

Maria Mitchell was the first American to discover a comet. The King of Denmark gave her a gold medal because of her find. Maria was the first American to get a medal of this kind and the first woman astronomer to get any medal for a discovery.

Maria Mitchell became famous. But that was not important to her. What she cared most about was her work. She wrote a small but important book that helped sailors find their way by the stars. For many years she was a college teacher. For almost sixty years Maria kept learning and teaching about the skies.

Today you can visit Maria Mitchell's house on Nantucket Island. It was once the home of a girl who loved the stars and became one of America's greatest astronomers.

Discovering Dinosaurs

by GLENN O. BLOUGH

When you tell somebody that something happened a long time ago, you may mean that it happened a few years ago. Or you may mean that it happened before you were born or even before your mother or your grandmother was born. But when we write about dinosaurs that lived a long time ago, we mean that they lived a LONG, LONG, LONG time ago.

Dinosaurs lived on the earth millions and millions of years ago.

What did a dinosaur look like? There were thousands of kinds—some of them were true monsters, the biggest land animals that have ever lived on the earth, bigger than you can believe. People are likely to think that all dinosaurs were like that. Some, though, were as small as a cat that can crawl under a fence. And some of them were in between, not terribly big, but not small.

Dinosaurs were prehistoric lizards, so in one way or another, all of them looked something like the lizards you can see today.

Let's look at some of the biggest dinosaurs and see what they were like.

Can you picture six elephants, one behind another? The brontosaurus was as long as that, or longer. It grew to be more than twenty meters long. One fossil has been found that is thirty meters long. A brontosaurus was as heavy as all those elephants put together, too. Could you bring this dinosaur indoors? No; it would make a wreck out of your living room!

The name brontosaurus means "thunder lizard." We can guess that when a brontosaurus walked, the ground shook and a sound like thunder filled the air.

This stegosaurus looks dangerous enough to scare any trouble away. Look at its back and that great horned tail!

The stegosaurus was almost five meters long and three meters high, but like the brontosaurus, it had a very small head.

This monster has been called the king of the dinosaurs. The tyrannosaurus rex was sometimes close to twenty meters long. Standing on its back legs, it would tower above all the animals you know today. Just look at those teeth! How dangerous the tyrannosaurus must have been when it was angry or hungry!

You have just met a few of the largest dinosaurs. If you want to look up more about them, be sure not to misspell those long names! There are many good, readable books about dinosaurs—see what you can discover about them on your own.

Dinosaur Riddles

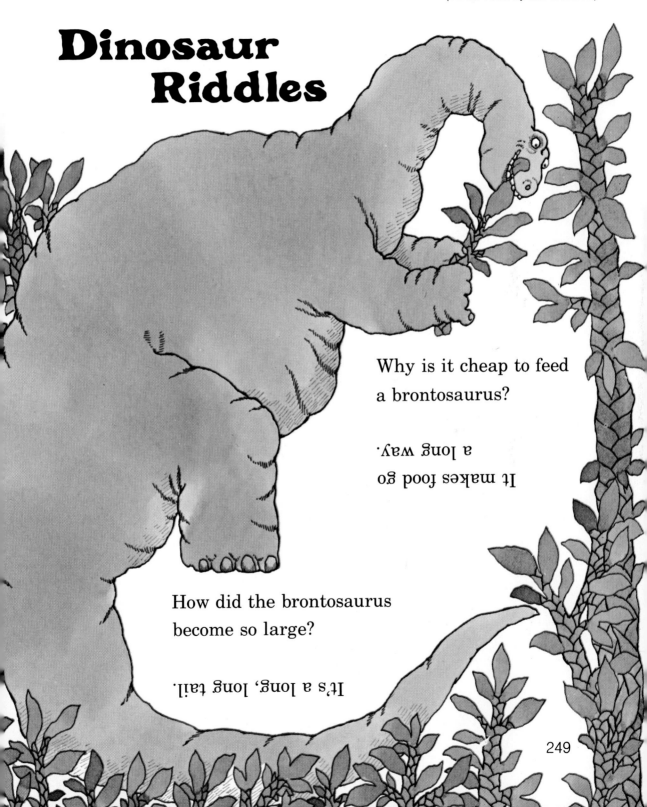

Why is it cheap to feed
a brontosaurus?

It makes food go
a long way.

How did the brontosaurus
become so large?

It's a long, long tail.

249

If you had a Tyrannosaurus Rex for a pet, where would it sleep?

Wherever it wanted to.

What is the dinosaurs' favorite baseball team?

The Giants.

What did one stegosaurus say to the other stegosaurus?

Nothing. Dinosaurs can't talk.

Why Writers Write

Writers write for many different reasons.
Here are some of the main ones:

1. to teach about things

2. to give enjoyment

3. to make people believe something

Look at the picture below.

Why is the boy writing?

Most of the selections in "Wonders of the World" were written to *teach about things.*

When you read that kind of writing, you need to read carefully. You must watch out for details. There may be things you have to stop and think about.

You may also have to study a picture or a diagram.

Now think back to the stories in "Wonders of the World." Can you remember one that you had to read carefully because it told you how to make something?

Can you think of one that gave facts about a person's life?

Which story gave you many facts about a place in the United States?

Some stories are written to give enjoyment. You do not need to read these stories as carefully as stories of fact. Read the following story. It was written for enjoyment.

When you have a last name like mine, you can get into a lot of trouble. My last name is Noe, and it sounds just like the word *no.*

On the first day of school last year, the teacher asked me to tell the class my last name. Of course, I said "Noe." Wow, did he get mad!

NOE!

Did this story make you laugh? Can you think of some other stories in this book that were written for enjoyment?

Some writers want to make you believe something. They may want you to believe an idea or to buy something.

Newspaper ads and editorials often use "strong" words to try to make us believe they are right. Some strong words are: the *fastest,* the *best,* the *most beautiful,* and so on.

Read the ad on the next page. See if you can find the strong words in it.

"GRIN Toothpaste will give you the cleanest, whitest, and brightest teeth. When you flash your GRIN smile, you'll win hundreds of friends. Don't forget—smiles are "in," so be sure to use GRIN.

Can you pick out the "strong" words that the writer used to make you want to buy GRIN?

Now read the editorial below. It was written for a school newspaper.

It's wonderful that our P.T.A. made over $100 on our school book sale. But now what should they do with the money?

Our school's baseball things are the worst in the world. Everyone knows that. We need new bats and gloves more than anything. Everyone also knows that our school baseball games are the most fun we have.

We just have to use the money from the book sale to buy new bats and gloves. That is the only way to use the money.

Susan Mendez

What is Susan trying to make the reader believe? Does she write about other uses for the money? What strong words does she use?

Read the following paragraphs. Then write or tell what the writer is doing: teaching about things, giving enjoyment, or making people believe something.

1. Do you want to be the greatest? Do you want to hit home runs, shoot a hundred baskets, and race ten miles a day? Then you need POW. Start each day with a big bowl of POW. POW will give you the POWer to be the best!

2. Run, don't walk, to your nearest shoe store and get some super-fast Race Right sneakers. Then zip around the block and pass everyone on the way to school. Race Right: the sharpest, neatest, fastest sneakers you can buy!

3. Once I decided to surprise my sister on her birthday by baking her a cake. I did just what the cookbook said, slowly and carefully. Then I put the cake into the oven. I set the timer for one hour, just as the cookbook said. Well, just as the timer rang, my sister walked in. "Surprise!" I yelled, and I grandly took the cake out of the oven. But the surprise was on me—I had forgotten to turn the oven on!

4. This is how to make hard-boiled eggs. First, place the eggs in a pot and cover them with cold water. Heat them until the water boils. Remove the pot from the heat and cover it. Then let it stand for about 15 minutes.

Salt Boy

by MARY PERRINE
Illustrated by LEONARD WEISGARD

The thing Salt Boy wanted, only his father could give him. But asking for it, Salt Boy thought, might make his father be against it. Then one morning he asked for it.

He was in the trees getting wood for the fire, when he saw his father coming with a rope to begin the training of the black horse.

His heart began to jump in a funny way, like a grasshopper, and he went to the bent tree. There he could stand not far from the black horse and watch his father when he threw the rope.

The black horse was eating grass. Salt Boy's father walked quietly, and the black horse didn't hear him until he was near. Then suddenly its ears went up and its head, and it began to dance away backwards.

Still walking quietly, Salt Boy's father threw the rope. With no sound it went high over the black horse's ears. It slid down easily around its neck.

The black horse stood there, surprised, and shook its head as if a fly had bothered it. Keeping the rope tight, Salt Boy's father went close to the black horse. He talked to it and petted it with kindness. Then he untied the rope and let the black horse go.

It was then Salt Boy went to his father and, hiding his face, almost, with the wood in his arms, said it. "My father, will you teach me sometime to rope the black horse?"

Without answering, his father started to their house, and Salt Boy went behind him. Without words they crossed the red sand of the high place and went down the black rocks below.

When they came to the pen for Salt Boy's mother's sheep, his father stopped and waited until Salt Boy was beside him. Then he spoke.

"I have said it before, my son, that you must never rope the sheep of your mother."

Salt Boy wanted to hide from his father the shame on his face, and he looked at the ground and turned a rock over with his toe.

He was thinking that his father must know, then, what he had done in the canyon when he took his mother's sheep for grass.

Then his father spoke again. "Maybe, my son," he said, "when your years are more I will teach you to rope the black horse."

Salt Boy and his father looked at each other in a way that was strong. Salt Boy knew his father had asked without words for a promise, and without words Salt Boy had given it to him. That promise he thought he would keep.

In the morning Salt Boy took his mother's sheep to the canyon for grass.

Near the wash at the bottom of the canyon, the grass was green and deep, and the sheep ran on it, pushing against each other. When the sheep ran, the lamb that was littlest lost its

mother and cried, "M-a-a." Salt Boy lifted it and carried it with gentleness to its mother.

There was a tall, flat rock by the grass where the sheep were, and Salt Boy climbed up on it. From there he could watch the sheep, and if he turned around and leaned over, he could see the cave that held that thing he had found.

He remembered the morning he had found it there. At first when he saw it in the cave, he had thought it was a snake, and he had felt it with a long stick and moved it and turned it over. When the stick told him it was a thing without life, he had gone close to it, and put his hand on it. It wasn't until then he had known it was a rope.

He had pulled it carefully and slowly out of the darkness in the cave. Then he had sat on the ground and looked at it and felt it and held it. He had done that with it all day, until it was time to take his mother's sheep back up the canyon path. Then he had coiled it very slowly and put it back in the cave's darkness.

After that morning he had taken the rope out of the cave many times. He had learned to tie it well. He had learned to throw it without missing over the round gray rocks that were in the canyon.

Then one time when the rope was in his hands, and he was getting ready to throw it over a round gray rock, a sheep had come near. Suddenly he had thrown it over the sheep's head.

Now Salt Boy sat on the rock that was tall and flat. He was thinking about that first time. And he was thinking about how many times after that he had thrown the rope over the heads of other sheep of his mother. And he was thinking about yesterday and the promise he had given his father.

He might have stayed there longer, but his legs hurt from the rock that was tall and flat, and after a while he jumped to the ground. Then without planning it he went to the cave where the rope was hidden.

He could see it in the cave's darkness, and he leaned down to take it out. Just then a noise began coming from the sky. Black clouds were in it, and wind was coming from it. Then gray rain began to come, and soon gray rain was everywhere.

Salt Boy started to the sheep. Heavy wind stood against him, and to walk he had to hold big rocks and pull himself.

At last, that way, he came to the grass by the wash. The sheep were afraid and were standing close to one another. They were stiff, like things made from wood. Quickly Salt Boy counted—first the sheep, and then the lambs. One lamb was missing! The littlest lamb was gone!

Salt Boy looked at the wash, which was near. It was full of water that was moving fast, like a strong horse running.

Something was in the water by the flat rock, and Salt Boy leaned over to see it better. It was the littlest lamb, and it was kicking and trying to stand. But it kept slipping and falling, and then the water carried it.

Salt Boy tried to go in the water to help the littlest lamb, but the wind pushed him, and he fell. To get out, he crawled on his knees.

The rope that was in the cave, he knew then, was the only way he could save the littlest lamb.

Gray rain was still coming, and wind, and he held big rocks and pulled himself until he was near the cave. He crawled to it and got the rope, and then he held big rocks and pulled himself again, until he was back by the wash.

He tied the rope as fast as he could and threw it. He missed and threw again. This time it went over the head of the littlest lamb.

Salt Boy pulled the rope slowly and carefully until the littlest lamb was out of the water.

He lifted it and held it in his arms. It was lying very still, but when Salt Boy put his face close to it, he could feel the beating of its heart.

Something—maybe a sound—made him look around. His father was standing behind him. His father stayed there for a while, and then he said with quietness, "I watched, my son, while you saved the littlest lamb of your mother."

He still didn't go.

Salt Boy held the littlest lamb and waited. Then his father said, "Tomorrow, my son, I will teach you to rope the black horse."

Glossary

This glossary is a little dictionary. It contains many of the difficult words found in this book. The glossary tells you how to spell the word, how to pronounce it, and what the word means. Sometimes a different form of the word follows the definition. It appears in boldface type.

Special symbols are used to show how to pronounce the words. The symbols are explained in the key that follows.

PRONUNCIATION KEY*

a	add, map	m	move, seem	u	up, done
ā	ace, rate	n	nice, tin	û(r)	urn, term
â(r)	care, air	ng	ring, song	yōo	use, few
ä	palm, father	o	odd, hot	v	vain, eve
b	bat, rub	ō	open, so	w	win, away
ch	check, catch	ô	order, jaw	y	yet, yearn
d	dog, rod	oi	oil, boy	z	zest, muse
e	end, pet	ou	out, now	zh	vision, pleasure
ē	even, tree	ōo	pool, food	ə	the schwa
f	fit, half	ŏo	took, full		an unstressed
g	go, log	p	pit, stop		vowel representing
h	hope, hate	r	run, poor		the sound spelled
i	it, give	s	see, pass		a in above
ī	ice, write	sh	sure, rush		e in sicken
j	joy, ledge	t	talk, sit		i in possible
k	cook, take	th	thin, both		o in melon
l	look, rule	th	this, bathe		u in circus

*Reprinted from *The HBJ School Dictionary,* copyright © 1977, 1972, 1968 by Harcourt Brace Jovanovich, Inc.

An accent mark (′) is used to show which syllable of a word receives the most stress. The word *bandage* [ban′dij], for example, is stressed on the first syllable. Sometimes there is also a lighter accent mark (′) that shows where there is a lighter stress, as in the word *combination* [kom′bə·nā′shən].

The following abbreviations are used throughout the glossary: *n.*, noun; *v.*, verb; *adj.*, adjective; *adv.*, adverb; *interj.*, interjection; *prep.*, preposition; *pl.*, plural; *sing.*, singular.

A

act [akt] **1** *n.* A part of a play. **2** *n.* Something done. **3** *v.* Behave.

actions [ak′shənz] *n.* Things done; workings.

admired [ad·mīrd′] *v.* Looked upon with wonder and approval.

Africa [af′ri·kə] *n.* The second largest continent. Africa is south of Europe.

against [ə·genst′] *prep.* **1** Opposing: She raced *against* two other people. **2** In the opposite direction to: We sailed *against* the wind. **3** Upon: He leaned *against* the wall.

alphabet [al′fə·bet] *n.* The letters of a language. Our alphabet is made up of the letters *A* to *Z*.

aqueducts [ak′wə·dukts] *n.* Pipelines that carry water from far away.

---

add, āce, câre, pälm; end, ēqual; it, īce; odd, ōpen, ôrder; tŏŏk, pōōl; up, bûrn;
ə = a in *above,* e in *sicken,* i in *possible,* o in *melon,* u in *circus;* yōō = u in *fuse;* oil; pout;
check; ring; thin; this; zh in *vision.*

Arizona [ar′ə·zō′nə] *n.* A state in southwestern United States.

astronomers [ə·stron′ə·mərz] *n.* The people who study the stars, planets, and other heavenly bodies.

Atalanta [at′ə·lan′tə] A person in a Greek myth.

atmosphere [at′məs·fir] *n.* **1** The air around the earth. **2** The mood of a place: The room had a cheerful *atmosphere.*

autumn [ô′təm] *n.* Fall; the season of the year between summer and winter.

B

---

belonged [bi·lôngd′] *v.* Had its place: The book *belonged* in the bookcase. — **belonged to** Was the property of: This book once *belonged to* my great-grandmother.

billion [bil′yən] *n., adj.* A thousand million, written as 1,000,000,000.

Biruté Galdikas-Brindamour [bə·rōō′tā′ gal′də·kos brin′də·mŏŏr] An American scientist who studies orangutans.

bore [bôr] **1** *n.* Something dull. **2** *v.* Make a hole. **3** *v.* Carried: The horse *bore* two riders on its back.

brief [brēf] *adj.* Not long; short: a *brief* vacation from school.

brontosaurus [bron′tə·sôr′əs] *n.* A very large dinosaur that once lived in North America.

C

---

call [kôl] **1** *v.* Use the telephone. **2** *v.* Shout or cry out. **3** *n.* A visit: We paid a *call* on our friends.

Canada [kan′ə·də] *n.* A large country north of the United States.

canyon [kan′yən] *n.* A deep, narrow valley with very steep sides.

coiled [koild] *v.* Twisted into rings.

A coiled snake

collect [kə·lekt′] *v.* **1** Bring together. **2** Get a payment: Governments *collect* taxes from people.

collection [kə·lek′shən] *n.* **1** Things brought together. **2** The act of bringing things together.

comets [kom′its] *n.* Heavenly bodies that move around the sun, at times showing long, glowing tails that point away from the sun.

comfortable [kum′fər·tə·bəl *or* kumf′tə·bəl] *adj.* **1** Free from trouble; at ease. **2** Giving ease: a *comfortable* chair.

cork [kôrk] *n.* **1** A stopper made of cork used to close up a bottle. **2** The thick light bark of a kind of oak tree.

course [kôrs] *n.* **1** A path. **2** A plan for learning something: a history *course.* **3** A part of a meal served by itself: the main *course.* — **of course** Naturally.

covering [kuv′ər·ing] *v.* **1** Lying over: Snow was *covering* the ground. **2** Placing over something to hide it: *covering* a person with a blanket.

crater [krā′tər] *n.* **1** A hole made by an explosion. **2** The hole atop a volcano. **3** One of the holes on the moon.

Volcano crater

curtains [kûr′tənz] *n.* **1** Pieces of cloth hung in or over a window. **2** Cloths hung to cover a stage or movie screen.

D

---

deer [dir] *n., pl.* **deer** A swift, graceful wild animal. The male has antlers.

A deer

Denmark [den′märk] *n.* A country in northern Europe.

disappeared [dis′ə·pird′] *v.* **1** Passed out of one's sight. **2** Passed out of existence: The snow seems to have *disappeared.*

discovered [dis·kuv′ərd] *v.* **1** Found out about: Columbus *discovered* America. **2** Learned for the first time: We *discovered* that reading is fun.

discovery [dis·kuv′ər·ē] *n.* **1** A thing found out. **2** The act of finding out.

disproved [dis·prōovd′] *v.* Showed that something is wrong or false.

---

add, āce, câre, pälm; end, ēqual; it, īce; odd, ōpen, ôrder; tŏok, pōol; up, bûrn;
ə = a in *above,* e in *sicken,* i in *possible,* o in *melon,* u in *circus;* yōo = u in *fuse;* oil; pout;
check; ring; thin; this; zh in *vision.*

downstairs [doun′stârz′] *adv.* On a lower floor: They lived *downstairs* from us.

doze [dōz] *v.* Sleep lightly; nap.

during [d(y)o͝or′ing] *prep.* **1** In the course of: She scored eleven points *during* the game. **2** Throughout the time of: Days are longer *during* the summer.

dwindled [dwin′dəld] *v.* Grew smaller and smaller; shrank.

E

early [ûr′lē] **1** *adj.* Happening near the beginning: the *early* morning. **2** *adj., adv.,* Before the usual time.

eclipse See SOLAR ECLIPSE.

electricity [i·lek′tris′ə·tē] *n.* A kind of energy often used for lighting, heating, operating machines, etc.

elevator [el′ə·vā′tər] *n.* A large box that carries people up and down inside a building.

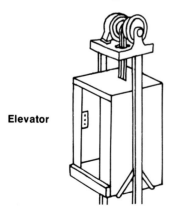

Elevator

F

fierce [firs] *adj.* Very wild or violent.

fixtures [fiks′chərz] *n.* Things fixed to the ceilings and walls of a building: light *fixtures.*

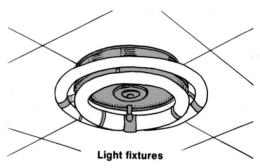

Light fixtures

flight [flīt] *n.* **1** The act of flying. **2** A trip in an aircraft. **3** A set of stairs: We climbed one *flight* and rested.

flippers [flip′ərz] **1** *n.* A seal's broad, flat limbs, used for swimming. **2** Broad, flat shoes, like fins, worn by skin divers.

formed [fôrmd] **1** *v.* Took shape. **2** *adj.* Shaped: well-*formed.*

fossils [fos′əlz] *n.* The remains of prehistoric plants or animals, hardened and kept safe in rock.

freight train [frāt trān] A train used to carry loads of goods.

G

giraffe [jə·raf′] *n.* An African animal, the tallest of all animals living today. It has a very long neck, long thin legs, and a spotted skin.

glossary [glos′ə·rē] *n*. A list of the difficult words of a book together with their meanings.

glowing [glō·ing] *adj*. Shining.

grant [grant] **1** *v*. Give. **2** *n*. A thing that is given: The king gave the brave knight a *grant* of land.

H

---

hammer [ham′ər] **1** *n*. A tool with an iron head, used for pounding things. **2** *v*. Pound or beat.

heart [härt] *n*. Muscle that acts as pump to keep blood flowing through the body.

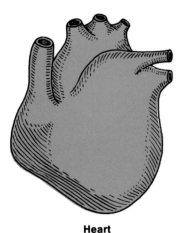

Heart

hibernate [hī′bər·nāt] *v*. Spend the winter sleeping, as bears do.

Hippomenes [hi·pä′mə·nēz] A man in a Greek myth.

holler [hol′ər] *U.S. informal, v*. Shout.

hummingbird [hum′ing·bûrd′] *n*. A tiny, brightly colored bird with a long bill. It moves its wings so fast that they hum.

A hummingbird

hurray [hoo·rā′] *interj*. A cry of joy or approval.

I

---

important [im·pôr′tənt] *adj*. **1** Calls for attention. **2** Has great value: an *important* book.

incomplete [in′kəm·plēt′] *adj*. Not finished or imperfect.

island [ī′lənd] *n*. A body of land surrounded by water.

---

add, āce, câre, pälm;   end, ēqual;   it, īce;   odd, ōpen, ôrder;   took, pool;   up, bûrn;
ə = a in *above*, e in *sicken*, i in *possible*, o in *melon*, u in *circus;*   yoo = u in *fuse;*   oil;   pout;
check;   ring;   thin;   this;   zh in *vision*.

J

joined [joind] *v.* **1** Connected or put together: *joined* two puzzle pieces. **2** Became a part of a group: He *joined* the club.

K

keeper [kē′pər] *n.* A person who takes care of people, animals, or things.

kilograms [kil′ə·gramz′] *n.* Units of weight. One kilogram equals about 2 pounds.

kilometers [kil′ə·mē′tərz *or* ki·lom′ə·tərz] *n.* Units of length. One kilometer equals about 5/8 of a mile.

kind¹ [kīnd] *adj.* Friendly; willing to help; gentle.

kind² [kīnd] *n.* Sort; type.

L

lambs [lamz] *n.* Young sheep.

lava [lä′və *or* lav′ə] *n.* The melted rock that flows from a volcano.

layers [lā′ərz] **1** *n.* Single thicknesses, or coatings. **2** *v.* Forms in coats: The artist *layers* paints. **3** *n.* The people who place something down: carpet layers.

library [lī′brer′ē *or* lī′brə·rē] *n.* **1** A collection of books, magazines, newspapers, etc. **2** A building for such a collection.

limbs [limz] *n.* **1** Tree branches. **2** Arms, legs, or wings.

loop [lo͞op] **1** *n.* A curve that crosses back over itself. **2** *v.* Form in a curve or circle: *Loop* the rope over the saddle horn.

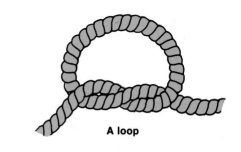

A loop

M

machine [mə·shēn′] *n.* A tool whose parts work together to do work of some kind.

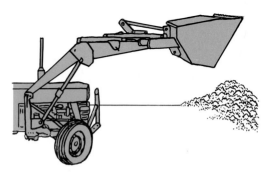

Machine for digging

276

marched [märcht] *v.* Walked with even, rhythmic steps: The band *marched* up the avenue.

material [mə·tir′ē·əl] **1** *n.* The stuff of which a thing is made. **2** *n.* Cloth or fabric. **3** *adj.* About things you can actually touch: The woman was interested only in *material* things.

message [mes′ij] *n.* Communication sent to another person.

meteorite [mē′tē·ə·rīt′] *n.* A part of a meteor that is not burned up and strikes the earth as a lump of stone or metal.

meteors [mē′tē·ərz] *n.* Pieces of stone or metal from outer space that are heated white-hot by rubbing against the earth's atmosphere. Meteors appear briefly as streaks of light; shooting stars.

meter [mē′tər] *n.* **1** Unit of length. A meter equals about 39 inches. **2** Instrument for measuring how much of something is used: gas *meter.* **3** The rhythm used in poetry or music.

Mexico [mek′sə·kō] *n.* A country in North America, south of the United States.

million [mil′yən] *n., adj.* A thousand thousands, written as 1,000,000.

mischievous [mis′chi·vəs] *adj.* Full of tricks and pranks.

misleading [mis·lēd′ing] *adj.* **1** Leading into a wrong judgment: a *misleading* advertisement. **2** Guiding in the wrong direction.

misspell [mis·spel′] *v.* Spell a word incorrectly.

models [mod′əlz] **1** *n.* Small copies of something. **2** *n.* Persons or things to be copied: a *model* child. **3** *v.* Shapes something: *models* clay into a horse. **4** *n.* Persons who wear and show clothes: fashion *models.* **5** *v.* Wear and show clothes: *model* the latest fashions.

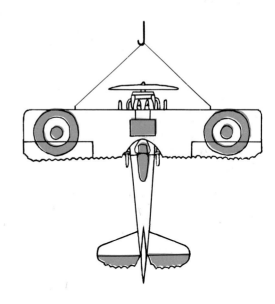

Model of an airplane

---

add, āce, câre, pälm;   end, ēqual;   it, īce;   odd, ōpen, ôrder;   tŏŏk, po͞ol;   up, bûrn;
ə = a in *above*, e in *sicken*, i in *possible*, o in *melon*, u in *circus*;   yo͞o = u in *fuse*;   oil;   pout;
check;   ring;   thin;   this;   zh in *vision.*

motion [mō′shən] *n.* Movement; a change in position.

museum [myoͦo·zē′əm] *n.* A place for showing works of art or scientific objects.

N

Nantucket Island [nan·tuk′·ət ī′lənd] *n.* An island off the coast of northeastern United States.

narrowed [nar′ōd] *v.* Became less wide.

national [nash′ən·əl] *adj.* Having to do with a whole country.

nature [nā′chər] *n.* Everything in the world, except for things made by people.

New York [n(y)oͦo yôrk] **1** A city in southeast New York State; the largest city in the United States. **2** A state in northeastern United States.

O

---

ocean [ō′shən] *n.* The great body of salt water that covers most of the earth.

orangutans [ō·rang′ə·tanz or ō·rang′oͦo·tanz] *n.* Large apes that have brownish red hair and very long arms.

otter [ot′ər] *n.* A fish-eating animal that swims and has a long, flat tail.

outlaws [out′lôz′] *n.* Persons who break the law; criminals.

P

---

patterns [pat′ərnz] *n.* **1** Designs; arrangements of things. **2** Forms or guides to be followed: dress *patterns.*

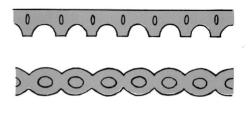

Patterns

pebbles [peb′əlz] *n.* Small, smooth stones.

Philadelphia [fil′ə·del′fē·ə] *n.* A city in southeast Pennsylvania.

platform [plat′fôrm] *n.* A raised flat floor: a speaker's *platform.*

plow [plou] **1** *n.* A tool used to turn over the soil before seeds are planted. **2** *n.* A machine that pushes through: snow*plow*. **3** *v.* Push right through: *plow* through the crowd to the street.

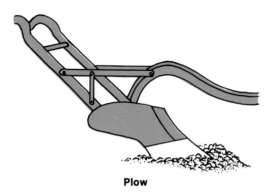

Plow

plowing [plou′ing] *v.* Turning over the soil with a plow.

points [points] **1** *v.* Is headed: The car *points* east. **2** *n.* The sharp ends of things: needle *points*. **3** *n.* Units of scoring: The team scored ten *points*. **4** *n.* Dots: decimal *points*.

power [pou′ər] **1** *n.* Any energy used for doing work, such as electricity. **2** *adj. use:* a *power* saw.

prehistoric [prē′his·tôr′ik] *adj.* Of the time before written history.

present[1] [*n.* prez′ənt, *v.* pri·zent′] *n.* A gift: a birthday *present. v.* Give as a gift.

present[2] [prez′ənt] *adj.* Now existing or going on: the *present* time.

promise [prom′is] *n.* An agreement to do something; word of honor.

Q

---

quiet [kwī′ət] *adj.* **1** Making little noise. **2** Still; calm.

R

---

recorded [ri·kôrd′əd] *v.* **1** Noted down for later use. **2** Stored sound on records or tape: *recorded* a song.

records [rek′ərdz] *n.* **1** Writings, charts, etc. that give information. **2** *v.* Round disks on which sound is stored: They played *records* and danced. **3** The best anyone has done in a sport: broke *records* in long-distance running.

remarkable [ri·mär′kə·bəl] *adj.* Very unusual.

rim [rim] *n.* An edge or border.

rocket [rok′it] *n.* A machine that can fly and be steered in outer space.

---

add, āce, câre, pälm;   end, ēqual;   it, īce;   odd, ōpen, ôrder;   to͝ok, po͞ol;   up, bûrn;
ə = a in *above*, e in *sicken*, i in *possible*, o in *melon*, u in *circus*;   yo͞o = u in *fuse*;   oil;   pout;
check;   ring;   thin;   this;   zh in *vision*.

s

scene [sēn] *n.* **1** A part of a play: act 2, *scene* 1.   **2** A place and everything in it: a charming country *scene*.

scientist [sī′ən·tist] *n.* A person skilled in some kind of science.

seals [sēlz] **1** *n.* Large fish-eating sea animals with flippers.   **2** *v.* Closes completely: *seals* the envelope.   **3** *n.* Special pretty stamps: Christmas *seals*.

secret [sē′krit] **1** *n.* Something that is not known.   **2** *adj.* Hidden; known by few people.

severe [si·vir′] *adj.* Hard to endure; harsh.

shapes [shāps] **1** *n.* The forms or the outlines of things.   **2** *v.* Makes into a form: *shapes* dough into loaves.

shirt [shûrt] *n.* A kind of clothing worn on the upper part of the body.

A shirt

short [shôrt] *adj.* Not long.

shrieks [shrēks] **1** *n.* Sharp, shrill cries or screams.   **2** *v.* Screams.

shrubs [shrubz] *n.* Low plants having many stems and branches.

Shrubs

sign [sīn] *n.* **1** A thing that stands for something else: X is a *sign* for multiplication.   **2** *v.* Write one's name on: *sign* a painting.

sink [singk] **1** *n.* A wash basin with a drainpipe and faucets.   **2** *v.* Go down below the surface.

solar [sō′lər] *adj.* Having to do with the sun.

solar eclipse [i·klips′] The covering of the sun's face by the moon when the moon passes between the sun and the earth.

Solar System [sis′təm] The sun and all the heavenly bodies that move around it.

somersaults [sum′ər·sôlts] *n.* Stunts in which a person turns heels over head in the air.

space [spās] *n.* **1** The area between two or more points; the area inside something: a cupboard with lots of *space.* **2** The area outside the earth's atmosphere.

spaghetti [spə·get′ē] *n.* Long thin strings of flour paste, boiled as food.

Spain [spān] *n.* A country located in southwestern Europe.

squeals [skwēlz] **1** *n.* Shrill cries. **2** *v.* Makes shrill cries: The pig *squeals.*

stalk [stôk] **1** *n.* A stem of a plant. **2** *v.* Creep up on; hunt: The lion will *stalk* a deer.

station [stā′shən] *n.* A building used by a group working together; a bus *station.*

steering wheel [stir′ing (h)wēl] *n.* A wheel turned by a driver to control the path of a car, ship, etc.

stegosaurus [steg′ə·sôr′əs] *n.* A large dinosaur that once lived in North America.

stiff [stif] *adj.* **1** Not easy to bend: a *stiff* felt hat. **2** Not graceful: He gave the king a *stiff* bow.

stop [stop] **1** *v.* Come or bring to a halt. **2** *v.* Hold back. **3** *n.* A place where something comes to a halt: bus *stop.* **4** *v.* Plug: *stop* up a hole.

stopper [stop′ər] *n.* Something that closes up an opening, such as a plug or cork.

store [stôr] **1** *n.* A place where things are sold. **2** *v.* Save; put away to use later.

strange [strānj] *adj.* **1** Not seen or heard before: a *strange* country. **2** Peculiar or odd: *strange* actions. **3** Not at ease: He felt *strange* when everybody spoke French.

sunk [sungk] *v.* Gone done under the surface of: The boat had *sunk* in the ocean.

T

---

tear [târ] *v.* Rip or pull apart by force.

telescope [tel′ə·skōp] *n.* A device that makes far-off objects look nearer or larger.

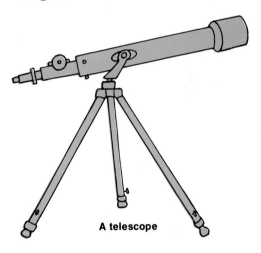

A telescope

add, āce, câre, pälm;   end, ēqual;   it, īce;   odd, ōpen, ôrder;   tŏok, pōol;   up, bûrn;
ə = a in *above*, e in *sicken*, i in *possible*, o in *melon*, u in *circus*;   yōo = u in *fuse*;   oil;   pout;
check;   ring;   thin;   this;   zh in *vision*.

281

thrilling [thril′ing] *adj.* Exciting; causing great emotion.

tide [tīd] *n.* The daily rise and fall of the surface of an ocean caused by the pull of the sun and moon. The tide rises and falls twice a day, or about every 12 hours.

tiptoe [tip′tō] *n.* The tip of the toe. — **on tiptoe** On the tips of the toes.

trail [trāl] **1** *n.* Something dragged along behind: the comet's *trail.* **2** *n.* A path, often through a forest. **3** *v.* Drag behind or leave a trail behind: The wolves *trail* their tails in the snow.

trapeze [trə·pēz′] *n.* A short bar held by two ropes, used for swinging through the air.

treasure [trezh′ər] **1** *n.* Something valuable that is carefully guarded. **2** *v.* Think highly of; value: She *treasured* the book she won.

trip [trip] **1** *n.* Journey or voyage: a *trip* to the beach. **2** *v.* Stumble: Don't *trip* on the loose rug!

twisted [twist′əd] *v.* Curved; bent: The river *twisted* through the valley.

tyrannosaurus [ti·ran′ə·sôr′əs] A very large meat-eating dinosaur that once lived in North America.

V

---

visitors [viz′ə·tərz] *n.* People who come to see a person or place.

W

---

walrus [wôl′rəs *or* wol′rəs] *n.* A large, seallike animal of the Arctic that has two long tusks in the upper jaw.

weak [wēk] *adj.* Not strong.

wears [wârz] *v.* **1** Shows or displays: She *wears* a smile. **2** Is destroyed over time, through use, etc.: *wears* out a pair of shoes. **3** Takes away material from by rubbing: Water *wears* away rock. **4** Has on as clothes.

weary [wir′ē] *adj.* Tired; glum and unhappy.

weight [wāt] *n.* The heaviness of a thing.

weighted [wāt′ed] *v.* Held down by the heaviness of.

whirlpools [(h)wûrl′pōolz′] *n.* Fast-spinning cones of water that tend to drag things down into them.

A whirlpool

282

whistle [(h)wis′(ə)l] **1** *n.* A device that makes a shrill sound when air is forced through a narrow opening. **2** *v.* Make a shrill sound by using breath, lips, tongue, and teeth.

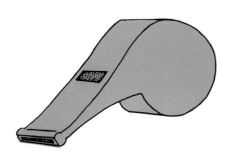

A whistle

whole [hōl] *adj.* **1** With no part left out: They spent the *whole* day in the airplane. **2** Complete; having all parts: a *whole* set of checkers.

world [wûrld] *n.* **1** The earth. **2** A great deal; very much: Your help made a *world* of difference.

wreck [rek] **1** *n.* Something ruined or destroyed. **2** *v.* Ruin or destroy.

wrist watches [rist woch′əz] *n.* Small timepieces on bands, worn on the wrist.

A wrist watch

Y

yesterday [yes′tər·dē *or* yes′tər·dā′] *n.* The day before today.

young [yung] *adj.* Not old; early in life: a *young* girl.

---

add, āce, câre, pälm; end, ēqual; it, īce; odd, ōpen, ôrder; tŏŏk, pōōl; up, bûrn;
ə = a in *above,* e in *sicken,* i in *possible,* o in *melon,* u in *circus;* yōō = u in *fuse;* oil; pout;
check; ring; thin; this; zh in *vision.*

New Words

Anansi's
Africa°
spider
even
god
though
grant°
marched°
tiger
course°
chase
able
tied
stalk°
short°
coiled°
shall
promise°

stones
broke
pebbles°
steel
sold
weak°
weary°
became
indoors
below

suddenly
become
matter

Atalanta's°
swiftly
flight°
anyone
against°
outran
marry
hoped
Hippomenes°
win
secret°
goddess
golden
apples
ready
shirt°
onto
behind
admired°
second

Tito Gaona
somersaults°
trapeze°
swinging
important°

net
platform°
steps
triple
family

spaces°
crowded
seem
counts
underground
power°
wires
electricity°
meter°
gas
hardly
joined
tunnel
without
shops
whole°
aqueducts°
milk
machine°
elevator°
playground
weekday

downstairs°
scene°

Words marked ° appear in glossary.

bouncing
clang
during°
miss
Tommy
stuck
understand
bore°
Mom
company
hurray°
creep
yell
noisily
holler°
drums
Ms.
yesterday°
bother
town

bottle
mail
message°
send
Roberta
aboard
ship
ocean°
mailboxes
Christopher Columbus

Spain°
sunk°
currents
kilometers°
stopper°
cork°
tight

lying
weighted°
Mark
mirror
island°
club
Tom
lighthouse
grey
tide°
eight
alphabet°
shore
sign°
fingers
lightweight
onshore

shapes°
lambs°
pages
autumn°
limbs°

cheerful
playful
child
speak

Ookie
walrus°
marine
trouble
salt
seals°
between
flippers°
actions°
decided
guess
bitten
tiptoe°
motion°
adding
finally
anymore

Dulary
face
Philadelphia°
wide
narrowed°
bottom
baby

kilograms°
Lewis
squeals°
shrieks°
nuts
thankful
stood
brief°
bananas
anywhere
shrubs°
lap
meantime
grown
thrilling°

nature°
backwards
strange°
wonderful
otter°
fun-loving
ski
pack
rat's
twigs
collection°
hummingbird°
feeding
body
leaf

Biruté
Galdikas-Brindamour°
orangutans°
forests
Borneo
Rod
scientist°
orangs
Ape
learn
arms
groups
disappeared°
discovered°
disproved°
mischievous°
hut
Sugito
kiss
ink
gnawed
pills
socks
sprayed
wreck°

itself
comfortable°
shaky

fierce°
giraffe°
neck
knees
woodland
doze°
lively
hibernate°
severe°
deer°
hearts°
chipmunks
bodies
sunny

dishes
kept
station°
till
dirty
pile
sink°
began
pans
flowerpots
fixtures°
hidden
outdoors
dried
belonged°

shooting
meteors°
outer
atmosphere°
completely
meteorite°
crater°
Arizona°
prehistoric°
Canada°
disbelief
museum°
New York°
incomplete°
misleading°
patterns°

comets°
rocket°
trail°
loop°
Solar System°
loosely
stony
material°
dust

colorfully
nine
points°
pressure
telescope°
Halley's
Edmund
recorded°
records°

Mitchell
eclipse°
covering°
notebook
Nantucket°
joyous
famous
astronomers°
interested
position
enjoyable
sixteen
librarian
library°
housework
remarkable°

Denmark°
college
sixty
visit

born
likely
brontosaurus°
thirty
stegosaurus°
dangerous
tyrannosaurus°
misspell°
readable

slid
kindness
untied
shame
lifted
gentleness
slipping
beating
quietness